Y0-BQJ-550

Simon & Schuster's

Guide to
SHRUBS
AND VINES
and other small ornamentals

Costanza Lunardi

SIMON AND SCHUSTER
New York London Toronto Sydney Tokyo

Acknowledgment
The Publisher wishes to thank Mr. Paghera, an architect from Lonato, Brescia,
Italy, for his kind help with the drafting of the two garden plans on pages 22–3
and 25–6.

Copyright © 1987 Arnoldo Mondadori Editore S.p.A., Milan
English translation copyright © 1988 Arnoldo Mondadori Editore S.p.A., Milan
English translation by Sylvia Mulcahy

All rights reserved
including the right of reproduction
in whole or in part in any form

Simon and Schuster/Fireside Books,
Published by Simon & Schuster Inc.
Simon & Schuster Building
Rockefeller Center
1230 Avenue of the Americas
New York, New York 10020

SIMON AND SCHUSTER, FIRESIDE, and colophons are registered
trademarks of Simon & Schuster Inc.

Originally published in Italy in October, 1987, by Arnoldo Mondadori Editore
S.p.A., Milan, as *Arbusti e alberelli*

Symbols by Daniela Carli
Drawings by Uwe Thürnau

Printed and bound in Spain by Artes Graficas Toledo
D. L. TO: 726-1988
10 9 8 7 6 5 4 3 2 1
10 9 8 7 6 5 4 3 2 1 Pbk.

Library of Congress Cataloging in Publication Data

Lunardi, Costanza.
    [Arbusti e alberelli. English]
    Simon & Schuster's guide to shrubs and vines and other small
    ornamentals / Costanza Lunardi : [English translation by Sylvia
    Mulcahy].
    p.   cm.
    Translation of: Arbusti e alberelli.
    Bibliography: p.
    Includes index.
    1. Ornamental shrubs. 2. Ornamental climbing plants. 3. Plants,
    Ornamental. 4. Landscape gardening. I. Title. II. Title: Simon
    and Schuster's guide to shrubs and vines and other small
    ornamentals.
    SB435.L8713 1988   88-11326
    635.9'76--dc19   CIP
ISBN: 0-671-66932-X
        0-671-66933-8 Pbk.

CONTENTS

ZONES OF PLANT HARDINESS

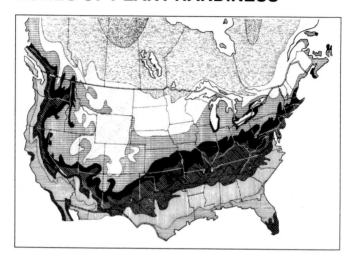

Approximate range of average annual minimum temperatures for each zone.

Zone 1　Below −50°F (−45°C)

Zone 2　−50°F to −35°F (−45°C to −37°C)

Zone 3　−35°F to −20°F (−37°C to −28°C)

Zone 4　−20°F to −10°F (−28°C to −23°C)

Zone 5　−10°F to −5°F (−23°C to −20.5°C)

Zone 6　−5°F to 5°F (−20.5°C to −15°C)

Zone 7　5°F to 10°F (−15°C to −12°C)

Zone 8　10°F to 20°F (−12°C to −6.5°C)

Zone 9　20°F to 30°F (−6.5°C to −1°C)

Zone 10　30°F to 40°F (−1°C to −4.5°C)

The above map gives a general indication of the zones of plant hardiness in the United States, given at the top right of each individual plant entry in this book. The zone system is explained more fully on pages 43–4 of the introduction.

Most of the British Isles falls in zone 8, with the exception of coastal areas in southern and western England, Wales and Scotland and all but the eastern coast of Ireland, which are in zone 9.

KEY TO SYMBOLS

flowering
period

fruiting
period

water
sparingly

water
moderately

water
generously

site in
full sun

site in
semishade

site in
shade

difficult
to grow

easy
to grow

WHAT IT MEANS TO HAVE A GARDEN

The role of the garden has inevitably changed considerably as a result of the constraints placed on it by modern society. As cities and towns have grown in size the amount of space available has decreased and gardens have tended to become smaller. Moreover, because the average homeowner cannot afford to pay a gardener to work his plot of land for him he has to do this himself in any free time he has, thus gardening, rather than being a full-time occupation, has developed as a leisure pursuit. It is nowadays regarded merely as a marginal occupation, a hobby that helps to make the home environment more attractive and comfortable.

A garden, however, is an experience in itself and can have a very deep effect on the lives of those who work it. Through direct contact with the earth the gardener can learn more about nature, the weather and the biological cycles of plants, and, putting into use the knowledge he has acquired, he will eventually be able to experiment with growing different types of plant.

Through the evocative power of the garden, its colors and perfumes, we can recall the first impressions of childhood. It is at this stage in our lives, between infancy and adulthood, that memories are sown and we first become aware that other creatures, such as insects and birds, move among the plants and grasses to make the garden a living entity continually growing and changing. This is reflected by the greatest 20th-century Chinese writer Lu Xun in *The Garden of a Hundred Plants*: "Behind my house there was a large garden, traditionally called 'the garden of a hundred plants'; when I was small it was my paradise. I cannot begin to tell you about the beds of vegetables, or the slippery stone of the wellhead, or the great honeylocust tree, or the deep purple mulberries, or the stout little bees among the rape flowers, or the ageratums or the skylarks that suddenly shot like arrows from the grass to the sky."

Although we live today in a primarily industrial society, we cannot forget the long agricultural tradition that is our past. Our forebears lived off the land, their lives spent in hard work, constantly struggling for survival, and although they had gardens and cultivated a variety of plants, these were for food and not decoration. The large ornamental gardens we connect with the past were the prerogative of the aristocracy and of the religious orders, privileged, elitist sections of the population with time enough to reflect on life, read, write and, above all, concern themselves with all that was beautiful. Thus, by good fortune, elegant, decorative gardens became a feature of the large stately houses of the noble, and these were commonly represented in the art and literature of the time. The aim was purely to provide entertainment and pleasure: some gardens had mazes in them whereas others were intended for leisurely strolls and the observation of the beauty of nature.

The spacious monastery gardens and grand, prosperous gardens of the nobles and princes were, however, poles apart from those at the other end of the social scale, belonging to the laboring cottagers who had to concentrate more on produce than on decoration. Gradually, however, as the agricultural society was overtaken by

A spectacular display of rhododendrons. Several of these brightly colored shrubs can be planted together to form hedges or shrubberies. Especially suitable for gardens are: R. yakushimanum, ideal for a cool or rocky corner; R. lutescens, yellow; R. augustinii and R. impeditum, violet.

industry, a new middle class was born which sought to emulate, although on a much smaller scale, the grand gardens of the aristocracy. At the beginning of the twentieth century, as cities continued to grow in size, the middle classes tended to move to the suburbs, living in small houses, each with its own plot of land. Although they were still interested in producing vegetables, they began, to think about the appearance of the garden; their awareness of ornamental plants increased and new and different species were gradually introduced. Eventually, the practice of growing food alongside showy, more decorative plants became the norm and the modern, well-planned suburban garden came into being.

Many gardens are still cultivated purely for ornamental purposes, however, these can look rather characterless unless they have been developed around an existing feature. A big tree such as a yew or cedar of Lebanon, for example, can create its own particular atmosphere that will totally transform an otherwise dreary area.

Gardens that have been newly planted or refurbished at the same time as the houses with which they are connected often tend to be rather impersonal. This is because their design and organization are all too often entrusted either to a landscape architect or, in the majority of cases, to the nearest nurseryman. As a result, the whole area is developed in a few days or weeks; loads of topsoil are brought in, plants are rapidly set in place, turf is laid over the bare areas and the garden is finished with the same speed one might fit out a modern kitchen. A garden, however, unlike the kitchen, does not have to be merely functional and practical; it should be decorative and pleasing

A Japanese garden in Kyoto. In contrast to the western garden, which is organized according to architectural rules, the Japanese garden is created as a "religious" experience, following a tradition thousands of years old. It is a place of serenity and

beauty, a microcosm of elements, each one having a life of its own. Here the emphasis is on evergreen plants, which offer beauty in every season; they are immaculately pruned and shaped by hand.

to the eye. This is why so many gardens, casually assembled by a commercial gardener or nurseryman whose main concern is to fill the soil, remain impersonal and aseptic. How much better if each garden were the product of the owner's care and his or her own botanical and naturalistic research – in other words, the work of those who will be living with it and enjoying it. Instead of hiring a technical expert to rush a garden through to completion, it is far better to put up with an unfinished garden that has empty spaces awaiting just the right plants. This gives time for reflection, time to consider the whole space in relation to its natural scenery. There may be some way in which the surroundings can be echoed and brought within the garden, some way in which a rapport can be established between old and new. In the long term, a superficial and hasty approach offers no return and a purely ornamental effect soon begins to pall. A garden is too important to be reduced simply to a decorative "packaged" deal that remains just as it is without evolving or developing. Instead it should grow with us, undergoing constant changes, never being the same. A garden is part of the living world, a dynamic microcosm, bringing with it continual surprises, pleasures and even disappointments. It is the ground, literally and metaphorically, in which mistakes (so necessary for progress), discoveries and experiments can all be made.

Like the verse of a poem or a musical phrase, a garden responds to our nobler spirit, to our contemplative, imaginative self. It is a place in which we can dream, and our wildest imagination can run riot among the sweet scents, colors, tinkling water, flowers and berries. It is, therefore, important that the basic design contains all the elements needed to create the desired atmosphere.

When designing a garden, most people start with one that has no established trees, consequently, their first aim should be to develop a basic structure of shrubs, small trees and climbing plants. (Smaller plants such as bulbs and annuals are transitory and can be changed whenever one likes.) The purpose of this book is to present the reader with a selection of the most interesting and varied plants to be found in these three categories.

The place of shrubs in a garden

A garden that already boasts a fine cedar of Lebanon or *Magnolia grandiflora* occupying most of the central area, or a well-established, slow-growing linden, is a garden that already has a shape, and its direction is already plotted. Any space thus dominated in a small garden (small gardens are our main concern in this book) does not need a great deal of work or reorganization to complete it.

Small trees, shrubs and climbing plants should be chosen carefully, with the following criteria in mind: their aesthetic values, their seasonal characteristics, their positioning in relation to buildings and their ability to withstand local climatic conditions. Such considerations will ensure that the garden becomes a permanent reality able to stand the test of time; it will always have its own specific atmosphere, giving at the same time, a feeling of constant change and of mutability which adds charm to all gardens. The succession of flowers and leaf colors through the seasons suggests the changes that occur in life itself while the evergreens give steady continuity.

With a view to providing both the experienced and beginning gardener with a wide choice of plants, a number of rather unexpected examples have been included in the book. For instance, the section on ornamental trees includes *Cydonia oblonga* (Quince), *Prunus avium* (Gean) and *Mespilus germanica* (Medlar); although these may usually be regarded as suitable only for the countryside, orchard or kitchen garden, they well deserve to be reappraised for their intrinsic decorative value as well as their usefulness. Apart from these, other shrubs and trees have been selected because of their fine show of berries. Gardens not only come to life with flowers and foliage; fruit and berries make interesting features, too. Some like the fruits of the *Actinidia deliciosa* (Kiwi) and the *Ribes rubrum* (Red Currant) are edible while others, like the fruits of the *Euonymus europaeus* (Common Spindle Tree), *Viburnum opulus* (Guelder Rose) and *Crataegus oxyacantha* (English Hawthorn) are simply a joy to the eye.

Returning to the theme of the structural function of the garden, it cannot be stressed too much that plants thrive best when they have space around both their roots and their heads. The open, airy spaces created by areas of lawn constitute ideal conditions for most small trees and shrubs.

Climbing plants, on the other hand, fulfil a different, seemingly marginal, function. They define the boundary of the garden and give to the space within a feeling of privacy and seclusion that is essential to any area in which one may wish to be alone to think and reflect.

Hedges

Shrubs give great scope for making hedges to break up a garden; they are far better in this respect than concrete walls and metal, wood or plastic fences. A planted hedge is advisable not only from an aesthetic point of view but also functionally since it gives excellent protection from wind. There are, of course, several plant species that are particularly suitable for hedging. A garden near the sea, for example, not only suffers from prevailing winds but also from the salt in the air, which decreases progressively up to about 5 miles (8 km.) inland. *Tamarix tetrandra* (Tamarisk), which grows freely on sand dunes buffeted by the salty wind, lends itself very well to creating a windbreak that protects the garden.

Hedging shrubs with thorns make a thick, impenetrable barrier against intruders, their only drawback being that they need to be trimmed at least once a year to preserve a neat shape. When it is planted, the hedge may be composed of one type of shrub or, to make it more compact, of several types. In some of the great historical gardens, for instance, these are wonderful hedges that consist solely of *Viburnum tinus* (Laurustinus), which creates a delicately elegant effect with its evergreen foliage. By contrast, if *Berberis vulgaris* (Common Barberry), *Euonymus europaeus* (Common Spindle Tree), *Crataegus oxyacantha* (English Hawthorn) and *Cercis siliquastrum* (Judas Tree) are all planted together, the result is a very thick hedge with profuse flowers in the spring and a fine mixture of red and pink berries as the seasons progress. This gives the impression of a natural hedgerow.

There are some who would like to make of their garden a sort of

An impressive example of an Italian-style garden in which box, rigidly aligned in symmetrical hedges, creates pleasant color contrasts with the enclosed flowerbeds and intriguing network of intersecting paths.

experimental theater. For them the challenge would be to create a hedge that forms a barrier like a theater curtain while leaving small openings through which the stage and backdrop can be glimpsed. One of the best plants they might use for this would be the slow-growing *Poncirus trifoliata*; it is a deciduous, very thorny plant with showy white flowers in the spring followed by orange-like, fragrant fruits. An alternative, with a decidedly Mediterranean look, would be a hedge made with rosemary or lavender bushes. Both are easy to grow, need little trimming or feeding and are strongly scented (this is especially true of the lavender when in flower). Another good protective hedge could be created with *Corylus avellana* 'Contorta' (Hazel); its progress from thickly-leaved green in the summer to delicate catkins when winter ends make it particularly attractive. A fourth possibility would be *Ribes sanguineum* (Flowering Currant); this makes an interesting hedge only about 6ft. (2m.) high, with reddish-pink flowers early in the spring. Finally *Fagus sylvatica* (Beech), although generally classified as a tree, is frequently grown as a hedging plant and makes a good windbreak or screen.

Rosemary, lavender, flowering currant and hazel are all suitable for creating hedges within a garden dividing one area from another – for instance, the flower garden from the kitchen garden or the orchard.

A hedge should not, however, be regarded only as functional and can add to the beauty of a garden. It may be used to conceal ugly wire fences that are required to keep out dogs and other trespassers or to form a background that gives a sense of unity to the whole composition.

Chrysanthemums and marigolds form a colorful cushion. Korean chrysanthemums, which can be brought on in containers, make a very decorative border to a lawn. Petunias, begonias, marigolds and impatiens flower through to September, to give a continual display in the garden.

Garden paths

An important element in any garden is the paths that link one part to another. These may be surfaced with materials such as gravel, brick, stone, pebbles, granite chips or rounds cut from tree trunks or they may be mere tracks across the ground. Most of them, but especially the tracks, which would otherwise be more or less indistinguishable from their surroundings, are defined by edgings of plants, which, in the great formal gardens of the past, were occasionally embellished with statues and fountains.

The smaller plants used for edgings are generally annuals, perennials or bulbs the disadvantage of these being that they are impermanent and all too easily broken down by errant feet and lawnmowers. Consequently shrubs or trees are more commonly used, the choice of species depending on a variety of considerations: How high should the edging be? Should it be evergreen or decidu-ous? Do you want it to flower and bear fruits for added color? Do you want it to shade the path? How is the path used and will the edging plants be tough enough to withstand the passing traffic? Will the plants be easy to keep trimmed to size? How well do they respond to pruning? (Obviously, the amount of pruning an edging requires and the ease with which it can be pruned are particularly important considerations if the plants have thorns or tough whippy branches that might snap across the face of a passerby.)

A final important question is whether the edging should be continuous, like a hedge or whether a few plants spaced fairly far apart will be enough?

Undoubtedly, the plants most often used for edging paths (and driveways) are boxwood and privet, because they are dense, can be planted close together and are easy to hold to the desired size and shape. They are ideal for creating a continuous, hedge-like edging.

For the spaced edging almost any tree or shrub will do if it is set far enough back from the edge of the path so it does not require too much and too frequent pruning (that is, if the distance from the center of the plant to the edge of the path equals approximately half the diameter of the plant when fully grown). However, the more slender, upright plants such as *Hibiscus syriacus* and *Juniperus virginiana* (Eastern Red Cedar) or *J. communis* (Common Juniper) are preferable. Best of all – at least for some edgings – are the plants that form a neat, compact, floriferous crown; for example, the thornless citrus trees, *Camellia japonica* (Common Camellia) or *Salix caprea* (Goat Willow).

Climbing plants

Climbers have flowers and berries, sweet scents and a range of wonderful colors, and fine foliage. They are most often used to decorate or cover garden and house walls, sometimes being planted directly in the ground or else going into tubs or other large containers, especially on a terrace. But they have many other uses, too. Fast-growing deciduous climbers make the best kind of sunshade because in summer they screen out the hot sun while letting in plenty of air, and in winter they allow the brilliant, warm sunlight to shine through on to the terrace and windows below. Evergreen climbers – most notably *Hedera helix* (English Ivy) – make splendid ground cover and are useful for holding slopes and covering unsightly stumps or rock piles. Moreover, all climbers, deciduous and evergreen, especially those with lovely flowers, can be used to create shady bowers in which to spend an hour or two on a hot summer day.

Some people, however, seem to take a tentative approach to climbers. For one thing, the idea persists that they are difficult to grow. An even greater drawback in the eyes of many is that they are not self-supporting. This, of course, is not altogether true. Many vines are quite capable of climbing skyward without assistance when there is something nearby that they can climb on. The gloriously luminous red *Parthenocissus quinquefolia* (Virginia Creeper), and *Hedera helix* will climb up almost any wall or tree to which they attach their holdfasts. The magnificent *Wisteria*, like a number of other fine genera, will climb anything it can twine around and in some areas it can be seen on old trees everywhere climbing higher and higher.

Climbing plants do, however, need support to grow vertically or horizontally across an open space, and this has to be considered when they are used in anything other than a ground-covering position. Various problems must be solved, depending on the kind of vine. For instance, on house walls, most climbers put out stems that grow behind tiles and bricks or poke into any open joints they happen to encounter. This is generally more of a nuisance than a serious problem but some vines such as *Wisteria* and *Hydrangea petiolaris* (Climbing Hydrangea) are powerful enough to do real damage in time; consequently they are best planted at some distance from any building that cannot, in effect, fend them off.

Among all the climbers Bougainvillea flowers most profusely and is the most striking. However, coming as it does from Brazil, it cannot withstand frost and so cannot be grown outdoors in cooler climates where the winters are hard. It is interesting to remember that the true flowers are very small and yellowish while it is the large purplish bracts that create the display.

Plants that grow by means of aerial roots, disk-shaped suckers and other kinds of holdfast may become a problem on house walls because, if they are ever removed, they leave their holdfasts behind and these must be laboriously scraped off before the walls are painted. This means they should be grown only on walls that are never going to be painted. Another problem with these climbers is that they cling so tight to the wall and frequently form such a thick blanket of foliage that they hold in moisture and keep out air and thus, in time, may cause a wooden wall to rot.

A third problem presented by very large and heavy climbers such as *Wisteria*, hydrangea and grape is that they may eventually crush the support that is provided for them. Consequently, they should be grown only on pergolas and trellises that are constructed of big decay-resistant timbers and 10-gauge or heavier steel wires.

Despite these negatives, climbing plants are delightful and not to be avoided. One of the number that is described in this book, the *Actinidia deliciosa* (Kiwi), produces both flowers and edible fruits: if planted in groups of three – two females and one male – and the winters are not hard, the fruits are delicious. It can also be grown in decorative containers.

Another plant mentioned is *Jasminum polyanthum* (Jasmine) with its white, sweetly-scented flowers. Although it is not included in this book, the slow-growing evergreen *Trachelospermum jasminoides* is particularly recommended for its hardiness; it throws out long, thin trailing shoots and its little white flowers are wonderfully scented.

Of all the species of *Clematis* only *montana*, which originated in Asia, is listed in this book because it is the least difficult to grow and invariably gives excellent results. *Solanum wendlandii* is a climber of ethereal lightness with sky-blue flowers, but it dislikes a harsh climate. *Mandevilla suaveolens* (Chilean Jasmine) responds to a mild climate in an exuberance of tube-like, usually white flowers; it is at its best in a sunny position against a wall. *Bougainvillea glabra* is definitely for very warm climates, while *Bignonia capreolata* (Cross Vine) and *Campsis grandiflora*, in spite of their tropical appearance, are certainly hardier. All these climbers are, on the whole, easy to grow and give excellent results if planted in the right conditions.

The garden: two plans
In order to demonstrate the possibilities offered by small trees, shrubs and climbing plants in the design and construction of a garden, two plans of hypothetical gardens – one for sun (pages 22–3) and one for shade (pages 26–7) – are illustrated. The characteristic of the shady garden is that it is rare for the sun to shine directly into it – perhaps because it is dominated by one or more large trees or because it is shut in by walls or nearby buildings.

The sunny garden
In the plan for an imaginary very sunny, hot garden, two species are shown growing in full sun, close to the wall of the house that looks out on to the garden. There are several plants of the August-flowering climber, *Campsis grandiflora* with its orange-red flowers, and two *Punica granatum* (Pomegranate), which are rather similar to *Campsis* except that they flower in June.

On the other side of a wide path that runs between the house and the main part of the garden are some *Spiraea japonica* (Japanese Spiraea), a deciduous shrub that flowers from the spring to late summer, according to the species. Another species, *Spiraea arguta*, is particularly graceful, with its white flowers arranged along slender arching branches.

On one side of the garden the plan includes several small fruit-bearing trees that enjoy a sunny position; these are *Cydonia oblonga* (Quince) and *Arbutus unedo* (Strawberry Tree). On the other side, there are flowering shrubs such as *Hydrangea macrophylla*, a nicely rounded plant with light green oval leaves and pink or blue flowers from July to September. The beautiful sky-blue of the hydrangeas blends perfectly with the misty mauve of the lavender, which makes a delightful sunny-border plant with its strong scent and aromatic leaves.

On the other side of the path is a series of rosemary bushes with little bluish-mauve flowers; these thrive in a mild climate. *Impatiens balsamina* helps to complete a perfect color-scheme while the hardy, vigorous *Lupinus* rises in triumph with its showy, colorful spikes. In the background, towering above this colorful display, is *Rhododendron arboreum* with spectacular red flowers in May.

The shady garden
Just by the gate leading into the garden, *Clematis montana* climbs freely over the wall. This species thrives in the shade and grows quickly to cover a fairly large surface in a short time.

At the top of the path that runs down the middle of the garden are two *Viburnum tinus* (Laurustinus), the ideal "all-seasons" shrub, with evergreen leaves, pink-tinged buds and white flowers followed by metallic-blue berries. Over to one side are two examples of *Viburnum opulus* (Guelder Rose); these grow rapidly, soon becoming quite dense, and should therefore be planted fairly far apart. Then come *Symphoricarpos albus* (Snowberry) and *Paeonia suffruticosa* (Tree Peony), the former with its pearl-like white berries and the latter with elegant spring flowers reminiscent of old-fashioned gardens. As a contrasting edging the charming and free-growing *Impatiens balsamina* makes a fine display with its bright red, pink or bicolor flowers and glossy leaves from spring to autumn. A fairly tall evergreen shrub, *Osmanthus fragrans*, in the right corner, produces delightfully scented little white trumpet-shaped flowers.

On the other side of the path in the most sheltered part of the garden a grouping of *Hydrangea macrophylla* and *H. paniculata*, both typical shade-lovers. Toward the far end of the path there is a *Sarcococca humilis* (Sweet Box), a small, evergreen shrub, next to which are some *Delphinium* hybrids, often to be found in flower beds and borders because of their very decorative flower spikes.

Scented plants
When we see a garden, the color of the flowers – especially if it is bright and showy – strikes us first of all. But if the flowers are also fragrant, this is the feature of the garden that we are most likely to recall at a later date. Here is an odd but interesting phenomenon. If

On the preceding pages: A garden in the sun with: 1. Arbutus unedo *2.* Cydonia japonica
3. Campsis grandiflora *4.* Spiraea japonica *5.* Punica granatum *6.* Rhododendron arboreum
7. Impatiens balsamina *8.* Hydrangea macrophylla *9.* Lupinus polyphullus
10. Rosmarinus officinalis *11.* Lavandula angustifolia.

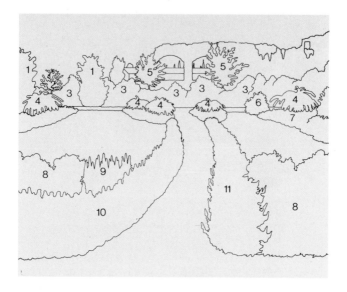

you are suddenly exposed to a wave of jasmine perfume as you walk down a city street, it is likely to bring to mind a garden you once visited in which the white-flowered *Jasminum grandiflorum* (Spanish Jasmine) bloomed luxuriantly. Smells are powerful reminders of scenes, events, people – the past. And pleasant smells delight and tantalize at all times. It is for this reason that, when choosing plants for a garden, you should consider their scent. Thereafter it is not difficult to arrange the garden so the perfumed plants can do their magic.

The positions that take priority when siting fragrant plants are near the entrances to the house, near windows and by the paths, from where the perfume can permeate the house, creating an illusion that the garden is flowing around us.

As the name denotes, the flowers of *Osmanthus fragrans* are perfumed. This, together with other more hardy species of *Osmanthus* (*O. delavayi, O. heterophyllus*) similarly with fragrant white flowers, is an ideal shrub for positioning near the windows of the rooms that are most often occupied so that the perfume can be enjoyed to the fullest.

If a pergola or gazebo in the garden is used as a sort of outdoor room, consider placing a fragrant climbing plant alongside so it will bathe the "room" with perfume. In a warm climate, *Mandevilla suaveolens* (Chilean Jasmine) would be appropriate. It is deciduous and cannot stand high winds or a temperature below freezing but can be grown in a large pot in more northerly regions if brought under cover in the winter. Hardier climbers are *Wisteria floribunda* or *W. sinensis*, the former blooming in early summer and the latter in late

On the following pages: A garden in the shade with: 1. Clematis montana 2. Osmanthus fragrans 3. Paeonia suffruticosa 4. Hydrangea paniculata 5. Delphinium hybrid 6. Sarcococca humilis 7. Symphoricarpos albus 8. Impatiens balsamina 9. Viburnum tinus 10. Viburnum opulus.

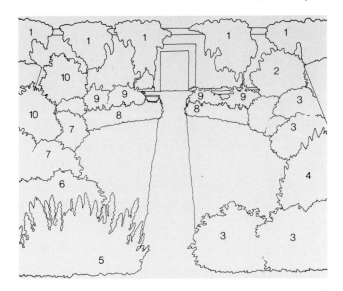

spring; their long drooping clusters of flowers are sweetly scented and look both ephemeral and spectacular when in full bloom.

Wintertime brings one of the most strongly scented shrubs, *Chimonanthus praecox* (Winter Sweet). This is a delightful plant that blooms from December until its leaves begin to show in the spring. It can be planted some distance from the house since at this time of year no windows will be open to allow the perfume to penetrate indoors but it will serve as an incentive to go outdoors every day just to savor its fragrance.

August and September bring the fragrant *Clerodendrum trichotomum*, which grows well against a wall, protected from the harshness of winter, but in sight of windows or doors as it bears beautiful blue berries on red calyxes. In February the hardy *Hamamelis mollis* (Chinese Witch Hazel) is covered with little clusters of yellow flowers on its bare branches. The May-flowering *Philadelphus coronarius* (Mock Orange) has earned its common name because of the whiteness of its flowers and their wonderful perfume. A similar perfume is characteristic of the hardy *Syringa vulgaris* (Lilac), which blooms in April and May.

In a position just outside the bedroom window *Jasminum grandiflorum* and *J. polyanthum* (the latter has twining shoots) will fill the room with their almost intoxicating perfume on summer nights. Similarly, the delicate fragrance of the flowers of the honeysuckle *Lonicera × americana* planted along paths and around windows becomes more and more enchanting on balmy summer evenings when it seems almost to hang in the air.

Chimonanthus praecox, *(Winter Sweet), is a very strongly scented plant that flowers very early, before the leaves emerge.*

Evergreens

When selecting trees, shrubs and climbers for a garden, one of the first decisions to be taken is whether you want an evergreen or a deciduous plant.

As a very general rule (there are obviously many exceptions), evergreens have darker green foliage than deciduous plants, are less strikingly floriferous and are much more inclined to be slender and conical in shape. A high percentage of evergreens, furthermore, are needled and have branches growing almost all the way to the ground. And of course evergreens are always green. These characteristics affect the way they are used.

Evergreens are ideal boundary plants because, like a high fence, they give privacy from neighboring properties and serve year-round as a magnificent dark backdrop for the rest of the garden. This does not mean, however, that evergreens should not be used well within the borders of the garden as specimen plants. Many of the needled evergreen trees – the conifers – are too large for a small garden, but there are smaller conifers, almost as handsome, that can be used in their place with splendid effect. For example, *Juniperus virginiana* (Eastern Red Cedar) which grows throughout much of the United States, forms a handsome spire that can serve as an exclamation point in a landscape plan.

Evergreens also make outstanding hedge plants in those cases where you want to hide an area or object that is unavoidably unsightly the year round. They create a good, sturdy barrier and make equally good windbreaks and snow-fences.

A very striking plant, Albizia julibrissin, (Silk Tree), has flowers shading from pink to brilliant red that seem to form a delicate pink powderpuff around the glomerule. Albizia species are similar to Acacia from which they differ only in that the stamen filaments are joined to the base.

On the other hand evergreen trees generally do not make good shade trees that you can sit under as the branches tend to hang too low and the foliage is too dense (the ideal shade tree is one that lets in a little light and air). But if your house and garden are so situated that the western sun is a blinding furnace in the late afternoon, evergreen trees or a tall evergreen hedge will provide an excellent sun screen by standing between you and the sun as it sets.

One place *not* to use evergreens is in the close vicinity of a swimming pool because they shed a lot of their needles in warm weather and these have a discouraging habit of drifting into the pool. They are much harder to remove from the water than large leaves.

Of the many superb evergreens described later in this book, several are worthy of comment here:

Citrus trees, commonly dismissed as little more than fruit trees, are, in fact, exceedingly decorative especially when young, with lustrous leaves and waxy white flowers. Although they are not hardy in a temperate climate they can be grown in tubs and used to decorate a sunny balcony or patio in the warm summer months, and brought under cover, in a greenhouse or conservatory, for the winter.

Myrtus communis (True or Common Myrtle) is a dense, rounded shrub for use in shrubbery borders and clipped hedges. It has glossy, green oval leaves that give off an aromatic fragrance when crushed. Like the genus *Citrus* it will not tolerate a cold winter outdoors but can be grown in tubs.

Chamaerops humilis (Dwarf Fan Palm) is particularly suited to gardens near the sea because its fan-shaped leaves allow the strong prevailing winds to pass through without damaging them.

Elaeagnus pungens and *E.* × *ebbingei* are hardy shrubs with leathery leaves. Both are resistant to wind, and the former especially is unusually lovely when the wind blows, because it glistens like silver. With considerable pruning, its sprawling informality can be converted into a fairly neat 4-ft. (1.2-m.) hedge. *Olearia erubescens* is also very suitable for a summer-flowering hedge. It is more tender than *Elaeagnus pungens* and is well-covered with white, daisy-like flowers.

Laurus nobilis (Bay Laurel) and *Prunus laurocerasus* (Common Laurel) are both seen quite commonly in gardens, the former having aromatic dark green leaves, and the latter, frequently grown as a hedge to provide shade.

Deciduous plants

Trees, shrubs and climbers that lose their leaves in winter follow the cycle of the seasons and, even after their leaves have fallen, have their own practical, aesthetic and decorative values. In fact, in winter, some deciduous trees and shrubs compete strongly with the evergreens to bring beauty to the garden. This is a truth that few people, even experienced gardeners, appreciate. The general impression is that trees and shrubs are attractive only when they are in leaf and festooned with flowers or fruits. Indeed, the garden editor of a famous home magazine once expressed deep disappointment when she discovered that an outstanding all-seasons garden did not have any plants with red winter berries. How could such a garden be considered a beautiful winter garden? she asked. What she failed to appreciate was that the garden, despite a lack of bright color, was made beautiful primarily by the interesting or sculptured shapes of the bare trees and shrubs and secondarily by the unusual bark of some of the plants. *Lagerstroemia indica* (Crape Myrtle), for example, is as handsome in winter as in midsummer, when covered with its crepey pink to red flower clusters. This is entirely due to its picturesque shape, the slender, sturdy, angular trunks, and its two-tone flaking bark.

But, of course, deciduous trees, shrubs and climbers are more than just attractive. As shading devices they are in a class by themselves because they cut off the sun in summer when we want to be cool but let it come through in winter when its warmth is appreciated. Furthermore, unlike the dense evergreens, they tend to give desirable dappled shade, and in most cases you can sit right under them since the canopy hangs well above the ground.

Unfortunately, some of the better known deciduous trees are today thought by some to be too big for the average small residential property. Many of these, however, such as the beech (*Fagus sylvatica*) and hawthorn (*Crataegus oxyacantha*) can frequently be grown as hedges, and there is no shortage of small ornamental species ideal for smaller gardens. There are also innumerable species of excellent deciduous shrubs and climbers.

Consider the dogwood family, the genus *Cornus. C. florida* (Flowering Dogwood), a U.S. native, celebrated for its white or pink flowers in the spring, profuse small red fruits and deep red leaves in the autumn, and graceful structure at all times. *C. kousa*, (Japanese or Korean Dogwood) is just as fine though slightly smaller. Its flowers are white, four-pointed stars that appear at the end of spring and start of summer; in many cases they blanket the trees so completely that the greenery is almost hidden. The fruits in the autumn resemble sizable strawberries. Another excellent U.S. native is *C. nuttallii* (Pacific Dogwood). And among the shrubs is *C. sanguinea* (Red Dogwood), which is particularly showy in winter when its branches are deep red. *C. mas* (Cornelian Cherry), on the other hand, is striking for its small clusters of early-blooming yellow flowers that appear on the bare twigs.

Corylopsis spicata is a delightful deciduous shrub with slender, flexible branches that are covered with tassle-like flowers in late winter. An ideal companion for it in the garden is *Chaenomeles speciosa* (Flowering Quince), which produces pink flowers at almost the same time.

Plants to grow for their flowers

Some people want to enjoy their garden mainly in the summer, so they concentrate on growing late-spring and summer-flowering plants. Others who leave home on long summer vacations try to have something in bloom during the spring and autumn. The ideal, however, is to have something in bloom more or less throughout the year so that there is always a colorful contrast with the evergreens and bare deciduous plants, the fruits and whatever other features, such as boulders, walls and sculpture, the garden affords.

In trying to give some indication of which plants are especially notable for their flowers, we here give examples to span the whole year. It is obvious, however, that the majority of plants bloom in the spring or early summer.

Prunus serrulata and *P. subhirtella* (Winter Flowering Cherry) make a spectacular spring display with a burst of pink flowers, almost like a symphonic overture to the concert of the garden. At the same time *Magnolia liliiflora* and *M. × soulangiana* come into bloom with their large red and pale pink flowers. *Acacia dealbata* is well known for its clusters of little fluffy yellow balls; in a mild climate it is one of the first plants to bloom from January onward. It cannot be grown (except in containers) in climates where the winter temperature falls below freezing and it should be planted in the shelter of a sunny wall. *Albizia julibrissin* (Silk Tree), with unusual feathery pink flowers, blooms later in the spring; like *Acacia*, it is a member of the Leguminosae family.

Sometimes certain types of plants are dismissed as having too short a flowering season and are thus omitted from many gardens. For instance, the flowers of *Syringa vulgaris* (Lilac) and *Paeonia suffruticosa* (Tree Peony) may fall within a few days of blooming if there is an unseasonal spell of hot weather. But surely it is worth taking the risk, because few flowers are more spectacular than the peony and none is so widely loved as lilac.

Tamarix tetrandra is one of the most impressive shrubs whether in a seaside garden where it is exposed to relentless salt winds or in a town garden where it thrives despite the dirty atmosphere to bring an

The jujube tree (Ziziphus sativa) *has a very decorative fruit in the form of a large drupe, like an olive, that is sweet and has medicinal properties. The tree is rather difficult to cultivate and makes very slow growth – it reaches a reasonable size only after twenty years.*
Nevertheless, it is a tree of extraordinary beauty with spiny, irregular and twisted branches and thick foliage.

air of elegance. It is particularly splendid when its slender pink flower sprays are glimpsed through a garden gate.

Cistus creticus (Rock Rose), with its single, five-petaled flowers of papery delicacy, is particularly suited to sunny, informal gardens. Between May and June *Kolkwitzia amabilis* (the big, fountain-shaped Beauty Bush) produces an abundance of pink flowers with yellow throats, rather like the foxglove. This is just preceded by the hardy *Kerria japonica,* with its graceful weeping branches laden with yellow flowers. Although not easy to grow, and suitable only for gardens in very warm climates, *Gardenia jasminoides* is spectacular for the classic beauty of its heavily scented blooms which gleam like snow against the glossy dark foliage.

In the summer months there are the white-flowered *Deutzia scabra* and *Myrtus communis* (Common Myrtle), the latter requiring a warm site. And although there is no shortage of flowers during the summer, *Nerium oleander* (Oleander) gives a range of cultivars and colors, in single and double flowers, that is hard to equal. Next to the oleander bushes – which sometimes grow so tall that, when pruned, they look more like small trees – could be put the charming *Plumbago auriculata* with its gleaming sky-blue flowers as well as the exotic *Hibiscus rosa-sinensis* with its large, rather unusual red, pink, yellow or salmon-colored flowers.

In a different kind of garden where the climate is both warm and damp – as may be found around lakes or near the sea – *Fuchsia magellanica* thrives. Its strange shadowy flowers are like little pink-and-purple Chinese lanterns.

In autumn many trees and shrubs produce beautiful colored berries often more attractive than the flowers that preceded them. The red-berried elder, pictured here, displays its berries early if compared with the coral berries of the common barberry which can remain on the plant until well into the winter.

Both *Caryopteris* × *clandonesis*, with its deep bluish-mauve flowers, and *Ceanothus coeruleus*, also with charming little dark bluish-mauve flowers but less hardy than the former, give pleasure in the autumn.

From June onward *Callistemon speciosus* produces a rather unusual flower like a small red brush.

A small tree that is beautiful in all seasons and makes a harmonious addition to any part of a temperate-region garden is *Lagerstroemia indica* (Crape Myrtle). Although it is not technically classified as a shrub *Chrysanthemum frutescens* (French Marguerite) is included in this book for its shrubby appearance. It is, in fact, a wonderful adornment to any garden with its attractive dark green leaves and white, yellow-centred autumn flowers.

Finally, winter also boasts a few flowering plants, including *Chimonanthus praecox* (Winter Sweet) *Hamamelis mollis* (Chinese Witch Hazel) and the long and slender-branched *Jasminum nudiflorum* (Winter Jasmine), which produces small yellow flowers on bare branches.

Plants to grow for their berries
The beauty of plants is to be found not only in their leaves and flowers but also in their fruits and berries. Many of these are brightly colored and interestingly shaped. Some attract birds, singly and in flocks, while others hang on the plants for months. There is a wide spectrum of fruiting plants from which to choose. One that is particularly effective is *Berberis thunbergii*. The flowers of this thickly branched,

33

On the opposite page: Camellia japonica, *a slow-growing small tree or shrub. Its exceptionally large flowers, growing singly or in twos and threes, range from dark red to pure white.*

thorny deciduous shrub are not very interesting but the little oval fruits look rather like grains of red rice.

Cotoneaster horizontalis and *Crataegus oxyacantha* (Hawthorn) are grown almost exclusively for the decorative value of their scarlet drupes. Another shrub that is grown for its decorative autumnal orange berries is the hardy deciduous *Hippophaë rhamnoides* (Sea Buckthorn); this thrives in windy, dry gardens.

To liven up the garden in winter few plants are more attractive than *Ilex opaca* (American Holly) and *I. aquifolium* (English Holly). These ancient evergreens, with their bright red berries, have been used for Christmas decorations for centuries. The latter, of which there are countless excellent cultivars, is considered a little more beautiful than the former, but it does not grow so well or so widely in the U.S. *Mahonia aquifolium* (Oregon Grape) is rather bushy and presents a fine splash of color during the winter with its clusters of dark berries that stand out more and more as the weather becomes colder and the foliage slowly turns red.

Sometimes, in warm areas, a rather strange looking shrub may catch the eye. It has reddish stems, large leaves and heavy clusters of fleshy berries that change from red to deep purple or nearly black and contain a strong dye. This is the sun-loving, evergreen *Pistacia lentiscus* (Mastic).

Another native of the Mediterranean is *Solanum sodomeum* (Apple of Sodom). This is a perennial shrub with spiny leaves and poisonous yellow berries in the summer. *Poncirus trifoliata* produces round, velvety, yellow fruit from October onward but these are almost hidden by the shrub's dense deciduous foliage. *Sambucus racemosa* (Red-berried Elder) brightens any garden in the autumn with its scarlet berries. *Sambucus nigra* (Common Elder) has black berries.

Plants to grow for their unusual leaves

Leaves are sometimes very decorative in themselves, either because of their seasonal coloring or because of their shape. The autumn foliage of *Cotinus coggygria* (Smoke Bush) provides a strikingly colorful display so, too, do the hardy, deciduous, shade-loving *Enkianthus campanulatus* with its wonderful reddish-gold leaves, and *Fothergilla major*, which turns brilliant yellow to scarlet. And then there is that favorite of hardy climbers *Parthenocissus quinquefolia* (Virginia Creeper), which, as it grows vigorously over the sunniest walls of a house, turns vivid red in the autumn before almost anything else. None of these, however, put on such an extraordinary display as the Japanese Maple (*Acer palmatum*) which is, depending on the cultivar, brilliant to deep red in spring and autumn and throughout most of the warm months. Furthermore the leaves are beautifully shaped and chiseled. In some cases, they are like small fern fronds.

The leaves of the evergreen shrub *Aucuba japonica* are flecked with white, while *Senecio laxifolius* has white-felted leaves.

Pieris formosa is a striking shrub with scarlet leaves that give it the appearance of being covered in flowers in the spring, when it also puts forth its white flowers, which are rather like lilies of the valley.

The leaves of *Mimosa pudica* (Sensitive Plant), are sensitive to touch and retract when even lightly brushed.

Plants suitable for a woodland garden

A garden does not always begin from a completely empty piece of ground. A house may be built on a plot that was previously woodland and still is populated with well-established indigenous trees and shrubs. Some thoughtless builders and home owners cut these down with the idea that the property will be improved with a whole new set of plants from a nursery. How much better it is to continue the natural theme, keeping the design flexible without any attempt at straight or geometric lines, following the dips and irregularities and, where possible, leaving the old oaks, maples and birches or whatever else may already be growing. By judiciously clearing away some of the undergrowth and weaker branches to allow more light to enter the area, or by adding a few appropriate plants that will thrive in a shady position and in woodland (usually acid) soil, the result will be a woodland garden.

There are some shrubs that are ideal for such a garden and are certainly more attractive in these surroundings than anywhere else. *Forsythia suspensa* is a typical example. It is enormously popular because of its abundant yellow flowers, which can be relied on to appear regularly in March and April. Unfortunately, however, it is often positioned badly – as, for instance, when it is made the central feature of a garden, for even when well-pruned and controlled, it is somehow out of tune with the leading role it is called upon to perform. It is much happier when simply helping to create the background setting. When used in this way among the natural trees and shrubs, it gives the impression of having drifted in with the wind and the birds,

thus continuing the general theme of the garden.

A small deciduous tree that also lends itself well to a woodland environment is *Laburnum anagyroides* (Common Laburnum). Its natural habitat is wooded mountainous areas where, in May, it is decorated with its large, pendulous yellow flower clusters.

Azaleas and rhododendrons fit very well into the woodland garden, too, since they thrive in semishade and acid soil. Whereas in a formal garden their decisive reds, pinks and purples sometimes appear to have an artificial quality, they look completely at home when blooming among trees or on the edges of wooded areas.

Cercis siliquastrum (Judas Tree) is also very suitable for a woodland garden especially when the young green leaves intermingle with the purplish-pink of its flower clusters.

Calluna vulgaris (Heather) grows well in acid, peaty soil and provides very good ground cover all the year round in woodland gardens. This dwarf evergreen shrub with pinkish flowers covers the British moors in the summer.

Euonymus europaeus (Common Spindle Tree) is a small plant that is showy in the autumn woods when its pink fruits ripen. Another shrub or small tree that is quite spectacular in the spring is *Salix caprea* (Goat Willow), with golden-yellow or silvery catkins.

The monochrome garden
At Sissinghurst Castle in the heart of the Kent countryside in England, the celebrated writer and gardener Vita Sackville-West created several small gardens in the 1930s. Among other ideas that she

experimented with was the monochrome garden in which all the plants were of a single color. The whole park consists of ten gardens including the tower lawn, the white garden, the rose garden and the spring garden. The white garden, far from looking cold, is based on the theme of light: on the play of light and shade, of shadows and of luminous details highlighted by the white touches in the garden, especially after sunset and at night. Vita Sackville-West skilfully used quantities of gray-leaved and creamy-white-flowered plants to soften the stark contrast of the white flowers against the surrounding dark-green yew and box borders. The effect is quite beautiful.

There are, of course, white-flowered annual and perennial plants that make it possible to have bloom in spring, summer and autumn. Among these are evergreens and deciduous plants, fragrant flowers and flowers that only open at night, as well as climbing plants for the garden and terrace. Elder, whitethorn and myrtle flower from April to June as does the white-flowered *Cistus creticus*. Among many others there are *Hydrangea paniculata, Paeonia lactiflora (P. albiflora), Syringa vulgaris, Jasminum grandiflorum, Deutzia* spp., *Philadelphus* spp., *Viburnum opulus* and *V. tinus, Symphoricarpos* spp., *Yucca aloifolia, Agave americana* (Century Plant, with enormous, spiny, rigid leaves and stiffly supported white flowers), *Clematis montana* and *Rosa × noisettiana*.

A garden for the birds and butterflies

A garden is not a real garden if, among the plants and flowers, there are no other features to help us enjoy and become more familiar with

On pages 36–7: At Sissinghurst in Kent, England, the romantic nature of Vita Sackville-West is present in the variety of plants and harmony of colors. She decided to dedicate a plant genus or color to each of the ten gardens that her husband Harold Nicolson, had wanted. This picture shows "the white garden" with Delphinium, Gypsophila, Eremurus albus, lilies and others; in the center is a bed of Rosa longicuspis, whose flowers have a very distinctive perfume. It is a tradition that, when anyone in the family marries, the ceremony

takes place under this cupola, which is completely covered in flowers.
On the opposite page: Nelumbo nucifera and Typhonodorum lindleyanum. When we think of
aquatic plants we are inclined to imagine great gardens full of shade with ponds and lakes
covered with water lilies and lotus blossoms. In fact, these can also be grown in a small
garden or even on a terrace merely by installing and filling a large plastic container with water
in a fairly shady position.

nature. Ideally, a garden should feature a pool or stream, with some appropriate plants, for there is nothing more relaxing than the musical murmur of water. But space is often a problem so music and movement must be brought in by birds, while butterflies delight with their colorful dances. It is not difficult to attract these winged creatures to the garden if you put in a few of the plants they like best.

Butterflies are particularly attracted to a handful of easily grown-plants. Their favorite is *Buddleja davidii*, which is why it is widely known as the Butterfly Bush. It is a tall, lanky, easily grown shrub that flowers profusely throughout the summer. Its long racemes range from dark purple, through blue, pink and red, to white. Other shrubs that are particularly attractive to butterflies are *Lavandula angustifolia, Viburnum* spp. and *Rosmarinus* spp.

Birds are somewhat more demanding. But it is not necessary to build a lot of houses to attract a large and varied flock that will call your garden home. (Some authorities, in fact, feel that many species of bird are becoming so reliant on the food they receive from humans that they are becoming unable to fend for themselves and, in some cases, are in danger of dying out.) By careful selection of the ornamental woody plants you put in, you can supply the needs of most birds for nesting places, food and protection from cats.

Birds that nest well above the ground have no trouble establishing homes in the trees, shrubs and climbers found in the average garden. For those that nest near the ground you need a dense "tangle," such as a thorny thicket of flowering quince, a big old shrub rose or a thick hedge to keep out unwanted intruders such as predatory cats.

The food preferences of birds vary considerably. Those that like worms, such as robins, or insects will appear in most gardens without any special attention. Others, however, will only be attracted by certain plants either for their flowers or berries. Blue jays, for instance, will often be found where there are oak trees as they compete with the squirrels for the acorns.

Most birds, however, like a variety of fruits such as those of the viburnums, mountain ashes (*Sorbus* spp.), currants (*Ribes* spp.), barberries (*Berberis* spp.) and junipers. Other outstanding bird-attracting plants are *Pyracantha coccinea* (Scarlet Firethorn) and *Rhamnus alaternus* (Mediterranean Buckthorn), *Aronia arbutifolia* and *A. melanocarpa* (the Chokeberries), *Ilex* spp., *Sambucus canadensis* (Black Elderberry) and *S. nigra* (Common Elder).

Thoughts about roses

In deciding which shrubs, small trees and climbing plants are suitable for the garden, roses must not be forgotten. A flower that is so evocative of literary and symbolic associations, of childhood stories, of feminine beauty and of the joys of romantic love cannot possibly be overlooked, and anyone who has a garden must find it hard to imagine being without the beauty and fragrance of roses. But the question is which species and which varieties to choose. Bush or climbing roses? New hybrids with royal names and stiff habits or old-fashioned shrub roses, that in May are almost bursting with foliage and flowers? In the section of this book in which plants are described with relevant details and photographs, it has been possible to mention only three types – just enough to indicate that roses exist! This is because so much has been written about these flowers that it would be useless to try to compete with all the volumes, booklets, brochures, etc. that are available. There is such a wide choice of type and color. Some roses have more than one flowering period per year. There are climbers or bush roses, some carry single blooms and others bear clusters. Sizes vary from miniature to cabbage-size blossoms. Some climb, some trail, some are bushes and some are so-called trees. There are also roses that are grown only for cutting and arranging in vases.

Fortunately there has lately been something of a change in tastes and a few professional rose growers are concentrating on reproducing the old-fashioned, species roses that were grown before hybridization became fashionable. These are the silent messengers that bring us the history of the evolution of the rose from the moment when the tortuous and mysterious genealogy of these plants began. It is, in fact, one of the most complex histories in botany. Examples of old-fashioned roses, so different in appearance from the widespread hybrid tea roses of today, can still be seen growing in many parks and in rose gardens surrounding old houses. Anyone who likes a garden with graceful, airy charm should try to find these old roses with their soft shapes, slender, curving stems and fine petals in delicate shades of mauvy-pink and creamy-white. There are many species but those that immediately come to mind are: *Rosa damascena* (Damask Rose), *Rosa chinensis* (China Rose), *Rosa centifolia* (Holland or Provence Rose), *Rosa moschata* (Musk Rose). *Rosa × noisettiana* (Noisette Rose), the Bourbon rose and *Rosa banksiae* (Banksian Rose) with its wonderful clusters of yellow blooms. This rambler is particularly suitable for pergolas and terraces.

Old roses need minimum pruning because their charm is in their casual, rambling quality. In view of the fact that they bloom only in the spring, the traditional flowering season, they are often rejected in favor of the hybrid teas that bloom from summer to mid autumn, but this is no reason to exclude their elegant beauty from one's garden.

So-called bare-root rose plants – those that are only wrapped in paper and plastic, without any soil around the roots – must be planted when dormant. The best planting times are either early spring or late autumn. Potted plants can be planted at any time from spring through summer and into autumn, even when they are in full leaf and blooming. In each case they must be placed in full sun and the planting hole should be much wider and deeper than the roots. It should have excellent drainage, because roses cannot stand to be waterlogged, and the soil should be mixed with plenty of humus. The pH should be between 6 and 7. If using bare-root plants, the roots should be well soaked in water before planting and then spread out fan-wise in the planting hole. Potted plants are set in as they are after the pot has been removed. Water heavily after planting.

Roses require less attention than most gardeners imagine. In late winter or early spring they need about a half cupful of general-purpose fertilizer. This is followed by a smaller dose when flowering starts and another small dose in early July. In very warm climates a fourth small dose is given at the end of August.

Wisteria is a generous, sturdy climber of great ornamental value with its white, pink, mauve or violet-blue flowers. It must be planted in a sunny position and pruned twice a year, in winter and summer, in order to retain the buds and eliminate the superfluous material. The plant is resistant to most diseases; it is long-lived, robust and bears many attractive flowers.

Aphids, also known as green-fly, are a common pest but can be removed manually or by spraying with malathion. If the first method is too laborious and you disapprove of the second, you can try soaking nettle leaves and stalks in water for a few days and spraying this solution on the plants. Another possible solution is to plant a garlic bulb at the foot of each rose before it comes into growth.

Some thoughts about citrus plants

Anyone wishing to introduce a few small trees into a new or established garden in a subtropical climate would do well to consider some of the popular citrus varieties. These include *Citrus limon* (Lemon), *C. × paradisi* (Grapefruit), *C. aurantium* (Seville or Bitter Orange), *C. sinensis* (Sweet Orange) and *C. aurantium* subsp. *bergamia* (Bergamot).

Goethe expressed his feelings well when, speaking of the Mediterranean, he asked: "Do you know the country where the lemon-trees flower/And the golden oranges glow in the dark foliage?" Few people can resist the temptation of having their own lemon tree even though it is usually planted in a container so that it can be put under cover at the first sign of cold weather. It can look lovely on a terrace, under an archway or just by the garden gate. To extend the idea, if you live where the climate is suitable, why not design a garden with citrus trees? Of all the citrus varieties, *C. aurantium* and *Poncirus trifoliata* are most tolerant of cold weather. *C. aurantium* is the Seville or bitter orange that is also used as stock for other types of citrus. In Europe, this small tree is often seen in public gardens and lining sea- and lakeside promenades because it is so decorative and because it bears heavy crops of oranges that look just like the sweet orange but are, in fact, too sour to eat; consequently, since no one is likely to steal them, the beauty of the trees is preserved.

Citrus trees prefer a fertile, open, well-drained soil with a good depth of topsoil; they do not thrive in clay or in dry, sandy conditions. The best time for planting is in March and May when the young trees should be given a dressing of potassium-phosphate followed by a nitrogenous fertilizer every year. Overfeeding reduces the plants' resistance to unfavorable conditions. The ground at the base of the trunk should be kept free of weeds by regular hoeing; chemical weed-killers should never be used. Regular watering is essential.

To ensure that lemons ripen well and to avoid misshapen fruit, fungal diseases and infestations of aphids, there is an easy precaution that can be taken which cannot upset the balance of nature. This consists of spraying with a solution made from tincture of propolis (bee-glue) – the substance obtained by bees from the buds of plants – in the proportion of 1 oz. (25 g.) to 2½ gal. (10 liters) of water.

THE POSITION OF THE GARDEN

Not every garden is sited on an absolutely flat piece of ground; usually it slopes down or up, or to one side or the other. This kind of ground may present problems. The worst, of course, is bad drainage. Preventing runoff water caused by heavy rain from cutting gullies through a hillside garden and carrying off precious topsoil takes considerable forethought and effort especially while the garden is first being developed. One very effective way of dealing with the problem of soil erosion is to plant soil-retaining shrubs.

Another problem of sloping gardens is that they are harder to take care of than flat gardens. Obviously, the severity of this problem increases with the degree of the slope and the age of the gardener. Even a young gardener, however, may find digging, cultivation, planting, tending and mowing of slightly sloping ground wearisome after a few hours.

Finally, the enjoyment of a garden from inside the house may be adversely affected by the direction and degree of the slope. For example, if your garden slopes steeply down from your house, you can see only the near part of it from a groundfloor window.

Despite the problems, however, sloping gardens have much to recommend them; they tend to be less formal looking than flat gardens and reflect the curves of natural countryside where straight, rigid lines are rarely found.

But suppose the slope of your garden area is not to your liking; how can you correct it? Short of bringing in, or excavating and removing, enormous quantities of soil, the easiest answer is terracing. This involves grading out the bank in a series of "cut and fill" exercises that you then turf or plant to retain. A steeper slope will require a suitably strong retaining wall of stone, concrete block, brick or timber, the advantage of these structures being that, unlike a planted slope, they demand no attention if properly constructed.

Selection of plants for a garden depends partly on whether it is flat, sloping or terraced. For example, if you want to obliterate the view of a tall building at the rear of a flat garden, you should plant somewhat taller trees than would be needed if the garden slopes upward toward the back. By the same token, a greater number of small shrubs will be required in a terraced garden than in a flat or sloping garden.

Plant selection also depends on the orientation of the garden. If it faces south, that is ideal because it is exposed to the maximum available sunlight at all times of the year, and most plants need sun. But there are, of course, plants that prefer semishade and a few that want continual shade; consequently, all is not lost if your garden faces north, east or west.

CLIMATE

Of all the factors that bear on the selection of garden plants, none is more important than climate. Climate is the product of the temperature, humidity, wind, latitude and altitude. You cannot change the latitude and altitude at which you live and you cannot do much about the temperature, humidity and wind; however, there are ways of modifying these slightly in order to permit you to grow plants that might not succeed otherwise.

For example, by planting a windbreak of hemlocks, privet or other good hedging material it is possible to break the force of the wind as it passes through and thus protect more delicate plants on the lee-side that would otherwise be damaged or even killed.

In a dry climate a pond in the garden raises the humidity slightly in the vicinity and can also be used to store rainwater needed by plants.

Planting tender plants beneath the protective branches of a small tree or shrub will help them to survive the first autumn frosts. Similarly by building a wall across a slope, you can divert the cold air rolling down the slope away from the plants in the low spot at the foot of the slope.

The most practical way to cope with climate, however, is to limit your choice of plants to those that are known to be generally hardy in climates similar to yours. To do this turn to the Plant Hardiness Zone Map at the beginning of this book, find where you live and note the number of the climate zone.

The climate zones are numbered from no. 1 in the far north of the United States to no. 10 in the south. Britain is generally between zones 8 and 9. In the second part of this book, the climate zone is given for each of the plants described. As an example of how the climate zone system works a shrub such as *Philadelphus coronarius* (Mock Orange) is described as hardy to zone 6. This means that mock orange, if planted in zone 6, or south of it will survive the cold winter months, but is unlikely to do so in zone 5.

Needless to say, these zones are intended as guidelines and just because the experience of many gardeners has shown that mock orange cannot be grown north of zone 6 there is no reason why you can't try it in your garden if you live in zone 5; it is possible that the plant might do well either because you are in a micro climate that is

A garden becomes more attractive and interesting if it is on a slight slope or terraced. The overall effect can be further increased by the addition of a few rocks or by the introduction of little springs or streams to form a pool or small lake. A well-chosen selection of plants will

also add to the appeal of the display: small spreading plants for ground cover, larger bushy plants for a colorful variety of flowers and shrubs and ornamental trees for their flowers, fruits and foliage.

warmer than the rest of zone 5 or because you have placed the plant in a high, sunny position where it is protected from the cold.

PRUNING

Pruning serves various purposes: to keep plants in a compact shape, to encourage the production of flowers and fruit, and to keep plants healthy. In some cases, pruning must be done very lightly just to remove any dead or non fruiting pieces. In other cases, hard pruning is necessary to stimulate flower production and growth.

The development of many plants is determined by the leading or apical bud which, because it grows faster than the lateral buds on the stem beneath, restricts the development of the latter. Thus, by cutting out the terminal bud you can make the side shoots grow more freely and the plant becomes bushy. To obtain an attractive shape, each branch or stem should be pruned back to just above a bud growing in the direction in which you wish to plant to fill out. Also, to get a really sturdy plant, it is advisable to remove any weak growth.

Buddleja davidii for instance, flowers on the current year's growth and so should be heavily pruned every spring in order to produce new flower buds. Deutzia, on the other hand, flowers on branches several years old and if it were pruned like *Buddleja* it would have no flowers at all. *Wisteria sinensis* should be pruned twice a year – in the summer to reduce the shoots to 6 in. (15 cm.) and in early spring to shorten the same shoots to two or three buds from the base so that the resultant spurs will bear flowers.

Pruning must also be done to protect the health of a plant so that it can grow vigorously. All diseased or dead material should be removed and branches thinned out when they become too profuse to enable the air and light to penetrate. Suckers springing from the trunk and roots should also be removed regularly as they sap the strength of the plant. If the plant is in growth and likely to "bleed" or become frost-bitten, it is advisable to spread a sealant over the cuts.

Most pruning is carried out at the end of winter or in early spring.

FEEDING AND FERTILITY OF THE SOIL

So far as methods of soil fertilization are concerned, all that is required is a basic knowledge of the various types of corrective substances that will improve the physical structure of the soil. The best fertilizers are organic materials such as humus, leafmold and manure as these do not upset nature's balance. Careless use of synthetic, inorganic fertilizers and pesticides can easily ruin the long term fertility of the soil. Manure, which must only be used when well-rotted to avoid damage to roots, should be spread generously at the rate of about ½–¾ cwt. per sq. yd. (30–40 kg. per sq. m.).

The presence of humus in soil is very important to its fertility. Humus is fertile organic material in an advanced state of decomposition and it helps greatly both to retain water and to improve drainage. It also helps to keep soil open and to feed the bacteria that break down the organic material. Even if the soil has already been treated with a number of chemical fertilizers, without organic material the majority of the essential bacteria will not survive. Humus-rich soil is dark in color and is better able to absorb heat than light-colored soil.

Leafmold is an excellent form of humus that everyone can make simply by gathering all the leaves that fall from the trees in the autumn into a pile and leaving them there until they decompose into a dark, crumbly, light-weight material that you work into the soil. Leafmold not only improves the tilth of the soil but adds a certain amount of nourishment, too. A supply of leafmold is also useful in a garden for the autumn mulching of less hardy plants.

Other materials that help to improve the texture and composition of soil are: peat, which comes from low-lying marshlands; garden compost, made from waste materials from the garden and kitchen which have been left to rot with the help of a nitrogenous decomposer; seaweed, which can be found in coastal areas, especially after the spring rains, and which contains a certain amount of nutritive material.

To assess the composition of your soil use a good soil-testing kit such as can be bought at any good nursery. In the United States gardeners generally prefer to take an actual soil sample along to the state agricultural extension service for an accurate analysis.

THE COMPOSITION OF THE SOIL

The soil should be regarded as a living, vital organism. It derives from the disintegration of rocks and consists of mineral salts and vital elements that are microorganisms. The various types of soil are generally classified as acid, alkaline or neutral, the degree of acidity or alkalinity being expressed by the symbol pH. The pH scale goes from 0 to 14 and soil is regarded as acid if its pH is below 7 and alkaline if it is above 7.

Acid soils are usually found in cold, damp, hilly or mountainous areas such as moorland where the alkalis have been leached away through the centuries. Conversely, alkaline soils are more frequently found in dry, calcareous soils in temperate regions, for example on wide, open plains. In this type of terrain the basic substances gradually come to the surface from the subsoil and the salts accumulate in the upper strata as a result of persistent evaporation. Each type of soil has its own specific flora. For instance, among acid-loving plants we find the heathers, birch trees, ferns, rye and potatoes while alkaline-lovers include tamarisks, beans and wheat.

In most gardens the pH levels range between 4.5 and a little over 8.5. A reading of pH7 means that the soil is neutral. This is the level that most plants prefer. If hydrangeas show a strong tendency to be pink, the soil is alkaline; if they are blue, it is acid. In order to reduce the acidity a good dressing of lime is usually applied. Apart from being a corrective, this increases the calcium content of the soil.

The task of reducing the pH of alkaline soil is more difficult. The best way is to dig in generous amounts of peat and other acid organic materials such as oak leafmold and pine needles. It should be

On the opposite page: Rhododendron arboreum *flowers from March to May; its dark red bell-like flowers are grouped in closely packed inflorescences. Here it has adopted the habit of a small tree, blending in with the surrounding woodland to create a natural environment that does not feel artificial or manmade.*

remembered that irrigation tends to correct the acidity of soil when the water is hard and calcareous whereas water that lacks calcium tends to deprive the soil of this element, and thus increase its tendency to acidity.

WATERING

To be of real value to plants, water should reach right down to the roots and not merely moisten the surface of the ground. In general, ½ cu. in. (1 cu. cm.) of water reaches a depth of about 3½ in. (9 cm.) in soil. Light watering during long dry spells does not reach most of the roots and a hard crust forms on the top layer of soil, causing the plants to put out surface roots. These are damaged in subsequent dry periods and the plants suffer. It is not enough to find out whether the ground is moist by merely looking at the surface. It should be tested to a depth of 8–12 ins. (20–30 cm.) and if it proves dry, then a good watering is necessary.

Most watering is done in the spring and summer. Autumn and winter are the best seasons for planting when a good watering-in is essential, especially as this helps the soil around the roots to settle.

Sometimes shrubs in a dry position or under a big tree can be too dry even during the winter because the rain does not reach them. These will certainly benefit from being given water regularly providing none is given when the temperature falls below freezing point as intense cold would damage the roots.

PESTS AND DISEASES – PROTECTING YOUR PLANTS

The best way to keep trees, shrubs and climbers from falling ill or succumbing to disease or insect attack is to keep them healthy. This means planting them in the right place and the right way to start with and subsequently keeping them well-fed and watered and free of damaged, diseased or dead wood. But even when you keep a watchful eye over them at all times, they may become sick and die. In this century in the United States huge numbers of great chestnut trees have been wiped out by a blight, in Europe the majestic elms are being destroyed by Dutch elm disease, and in Tuscany whole areas are being devastated by the cypress disease, which is killing the most characteristic tree of the region. In such cases the only solution is to replant with a different tree. Orchards in California have also been ruined by the Mediterranean fruit fly, which probably entered the country in a vacationer's parcel.

Such calamities are generally unpredictable and, even worse, their spread is often uncontrollable. If a tree is really stricken by a disease only an expert will be able to give advice on what to do. However, there is a lot you can do yourself before having to call in the experts: first make sure the plant is not ailing simply because it is being shaded out by bigger plants, give it greater protection against the cold, check feeding, watering and pruning and look out for obvious signs of pests on the leaves, buds and flowers.

Many of the pests attacking ornamental woody plants can be controlled by spraying. The trick today is to find an effective spray material that doesn't upset the balance of nature, which is already seriously disturbed, and will not have harmful effects on humans. There are a number of these and more are being developed every year. Pyrethrum dust or nicotine sprays, for instance, are old standbys for getting rid of aphids and other insects. Sodium silicate knocks out the microscopic red spiders. Propolis, a glue made by bees, is good against some fungal diseases. *Bacillus thuringiensis* helps to eliminate the gypsy moths that ravage the oaks and many other trees.

In addition to sprays, it is a good idea to encourage the presence in the garden of birds and certain beneficial insects such as ladybirds and spiders, which feed on insect pests such as aphids; frogs and toads, too, will help keep green-fly at bay; electric fences around some very rural gardens ward off deer that in some areas will do untold damage to trees and shrubs in one single night; beer baits on the ground attract slugs and snails that may riddle rhododendron and azalea leaves with holes; fruit tree grease on some of the twigs of fruit trees will make these too slippery for insects and birds, who will soon learn to distrust such a dangerous perch.

In other words, there are more and more safe ways to protect your woody plants when they are attacked by insects, diseases and animal pests. The best way, however, is to grow them well and keep a constant watchful eye on them so you can spot the very first symptoms of trouble.

The colored squares represent the colors of the flowers while the periods of flowering and fruiting are indicated under the months.

	Shrub	Climber	Small tree	Evergreen	Deciduous	Hot climate	Mild climate
Abelia floribunda	■			■			■
Acacia dealbata			■	■		■	■
Acer negundo			■		■	■	■
Actinidia deliciosa (A. chinensis)		□			□		□
Albizia julibrissin			■		■	■	■
Arbutus unedo			□	□		□	□
Arundo donax	■			■			■
Aucuba japonica	■			■			■
Berberis vulgaris	■				■		■
Bignonia capreolata		■		■		■	■
Bougainvillea glabra		■		■		■	
Buddleja davidii	■				■	■	■
Buxus sempervirens	□			□			□
Callistemon sp.	■			■			■
Calluna vulgaris	■			■		■	■
Camellia japonica			□	□		□	□
Campsis grandiflora	■	■			■	■	■
Carpenteria californica	□			□			□
Caryopteris x clandonensis	■				■	■	■
Ceratostigma willmottianum	■				■		■
Cercis siliquastrum			■		■	■	■
Chamaerops humilis	■			■		■	■
Chimonanthus praecox	■				■		■
Choisya ternata	□			□			□
Chrysanthemum frutescens	■			■		■	■
Cistus creticus	■			■		■	■
Citrus aurantium			□	□		□	
Citrus aurantium subsp. *bergamia*			□	□		□	
Citrus limon			□	□		□	
Citrus x paradisi			□	□		□	
Citrus sinensis			□	□		□	
Clematis montana		□					□
Clerodendrum trichotomum	□				□	□	□
Colutea arborescens	■				■	■	■
Cornus mas			■		■		■
Cornus sanguinea	□				□		□
Corylopsis spicata	■				■	■	■
Corylus avellana 'Contorta'	■				■		■
Cotinus coggygria	■				■	■	■
Cotoneaster horizontalis	■			■	■		■

Cold climate	January	February	March	April	May	June	July	August	September	October	November	December
					▨	▨	▨	▨	▨			
	▨	▨	▨									
■				■								
■						□	□				■	■
						▨	▨					
	□	□								▨	■ □	□
						■	■	■				
■			■	■								
▨						▨	▨		■	■		
				▨	▨	▨						
						■	■	■	■			
▨							▨	▨	▨			
			□	□								
						■	■					
■							■	■	■	■		
□		□	□	□	□							
							■	■	■			
						□	□					
							■	■	■			
							■	■	■	■		
				▨	▨							
			▨	▨	▨							
▨	▨	▨									▨	
						□	□	□	□			
▨								▨	▨	▨	▨	
				▨	▨	▨						
	□	□	□	□							□	□
	□	□									□	□
	□	□	□	□	□						□	□
		□	□	□	□						□	□
	□	□	□	□	□						□	□
□					□							
								□	□			
					▨	▨	▨	▨				
▨		▨	▨						■	■		
						□	□					
			▨	▨								
■	■	■	■						■	■		
							▨					
■						■						

	Shrub	Climber	Small tree	Evergreen	Deciduous	Hot climate	Mild climate
Crataegus oxyacantha	□				□		□
Chaenomeles speciosa	■				■		■
Cydonia oblonga			□		□	□	□
Cytisus scoparius	■				■	■	■
Daphne mezereum	■				■		■
Datura stramonium	□				□	□	□
Deutzia scabra	□				□		□
Elaeagnus pungens	□			□		□	□
Embothrium coccineum			■	■			■
Enkianthus campanulatus	■				■		■
Erica arborea	□			□		□	□
Eriobctrya japonica			□	□		□	□
Euonymus europaeus	■				■		■
Exochorda korolkowii (E. albertii)	□				□	□	□
Fagus sylvatica			■		■	■	■
Fatsia japonica	□			□			□
Forsythia suspensa	■				■	■	■
Fothergilla major	■				■		■
Fraxinus ornus			□		□	□	□
Fuchsia magellanica	■				■	■	■
Gardenia jasminoides	□			□			□
Genista cinerea	■				■	■	■
Hamamelis mollis			■		■		■
Hedera helix		■		■		■	■
Hibiscus rosa-sinensis			■			■	■
Hibiscus syriacus	■					■	
Hippophaë rhamnoides	■				■	■	■
Hydrangea macrophylla (H. hortensis)	■				■	■	■
Hydrangea paniculata	□				□	□	□
Ilex aquifolium			□	□			□
Jasminum grandiflorum	□				□	□	
Jasminum nudiflorum	■	■			■	■	■
Jasminum polyanthum		■		■		■	■
Juniperus communis	■			■		■	■
Kalmia latifolia	■			■			■
Kerria japonica	■				■		■
Kolkwitzia amabilis	■				■		■
Laburnum anagyroides			■		■	■	■
Lagerstroemia indica			■		■		■
Laurus nobilis			■	■		■	■

Cold climate	January	February	March	April	May	June	July	August	September	October	November	December
□					□				▦	▦		
			■	■								
					□	□			▦	▦		
					▦	▦						
▦		▦	▦	▦								
					□	□	□	□	□	□		
						□	□					
				□	□							
					▦	▦						
▦					▦							
			□	□	□	□						
					■	■				□	□	□
				■	■							
□					□							
■			■	■						■		
							□	□	□			
▦			▦	▦								
▦					▦							
□					□	□						
■								■	■	■	■		
						□	□	□	□			
					▦	▦	▦	▦				
▦	▦										▦	▦
■									■	■		
					■	■	■	■	■			
					▦	▦	▦	▦	▦	▦		
▦									▦	▦		
					▦	▦	▦	▦				
□								□	□			
□					□	□					▦	▦
						□	□	□	□	□		
▦	▦	▦	▦								▦	▦
					▦	▦	▦					
					■	■		■				
						▦						
▦					▦	▦	▦					
▦					▦	▦						
▦				▦	▦	▦						
▦							▦	▦	▦	▦		
▦			▦	▦	▦					□	□	

	Shrub	Climber	Small tree	Evergreen	Deciduous	Hot climate	Mild climate
Lavandula angustifolia	■			■		■	■
Leycesteria formosa	□				□		□
Ligustrum ovalifolium	□				□	□	□
Lonicera x *americana*		▨			▨		▨
Magnolia grandiflora			□			□	□
Magnolia liliiflora			▨		▨		▨
Magnolia x *soulangiana*			▨		▨		▨
Mahonia aquifolium	▨			▨		▨	▨
Malus floribunda			▨		▨		▨
Mandevilla suaveolens		□			□	□	□
Mespilus germanica			□		□	□	□
Mimosa pudica	▨			▨		▨	▨
Myrtus communis	□			□			□
Nerium oleander			■	■		▨	▨
Olearia erubescens	□			□			□
Olearia phlogopappa (O. gunniana)	▨			▨			▨
Opuntia ficus-indica	▨			▨		▨	
Osmanthus fragrans	□			□		□	□
Pachysandra terminalis	□			□		□	□
Paeonia suffruticosa	▨				▨	▨	▨
Parthenocissus quinquefolia		■			■	■	■
Passiflora caerulea		■		■		■	■
Pelargonium zonale	▨			▨		▨	▨
Philadelphus coronarius	□				□	□	□
Phyllostachys aurea	▨			▨		▨	▨
Phytolacca americana	□				□	□	□
Pieris formosa var. *forrestii*	□			□			□
Pistacia lentiscus	■			■		■	
Pittosporum tobira	▨			▨		▨	▨
Plumbago auriculata (P. capensis)	■			■		■	
Polemonium caeruleum	■			■		■	
Polygonum baldschuanicum		□			□		□
Poncirus trifoliata	□				□		□
Prunus avium			□		□		□
Prunus laurocerasus			□	□		□	□
Prunus persica			▨		▨		▨
Prunus serrulata			▨		▨		▨
Prunus subhirtella			▨		▨		▨
Punica granatum			■		■	■	■
Pyracantha coccinea	□			□		□	□

Cold climate	January	February	March	April	May	June	July	August	September	October	November	December
■						■	■					
□					□	□						
□						□	□					
▦					▦	▦	▦					
						□	□	□	□	□		
▦				▦	▦	▦						
▦				▦	▦							
▦				▦	▦							
▦				▦	▦							
□				□	□							
						□	□	□	■	■		
							▦	▦	▦			
				□	□	□	□			■	■	
						▦	▦	▦	▦			
						□	□					
						▦	▦					
					▦	▦	▦	▦	■	■	■	
					□			□				
□				□	□							
					▦	▦						
■							■	■				
						■	■	■	■	■	■	
				▦	▦	▦	▦	▦	▦	▦		
□					□	□	□					
▦												
					□	□						
				□	□							
				■	■	■						
				▦	▦	▦	▦					
						■	■	■	■	■		
						■	■					
□							□	□	□	□		
				□	□							
□				□		▦	▦					
□			□	□								
▦			▦	▦		▦	▦	▦	▦			
▦				▦	▦							
▦			▦	▦								
						■				■		
□					□	□						

	Shrub	Climber	Small tree	Evergreen	Deciduous	Hot climate	Mild climate
Rhamnus alaternus	▨			▨		▨	▨
Rhododendron arboreum	■			■			■
Rhododendron simsii	■			■			■
Ribes rubrum	▨				▨		▨
Rosa (Tea)	▨			▨			▨
Rosa moschata	□				□		□
Rosa multiflora (*R. polyantha*)		▨		▨	▨		▨
Rosmarinus officinalis	■			■		■	■
Ruscus aculeatus	▨			▨		▨	▨
Salix caprea	▨				▨		▨
Salvia officinalis	■			■		■	■
Sambucus racemosa	□				□		□
Sarcococca humilis	□			□			□
Senecio laxifolius	▨			▨			▨
Solanum sodomeum	■			■		■	
Solanum wendlandii		■			■	■	
Spartium junceum	▨				▨	▨	▨
Spiraea japonica	▨				▨		▨
Symphoricarpos albus	▨				▨		▨
Syringa vulgaris	■				■	■	■
Tamarix tetranda	▨				▨	▨	▨
Ulex europaeus	▨			▨		▨	▨
Vitex agnus-castus	■				■	■	
Viburnum opulus	□				□		□
Weigela florida	▨				▨	▨	▨
Wisteria floribunda		■			■	■	■
Yucca recurvifolia	□			□		□	□
Ziziphus sativa			▨		▨	▨	▨

	January	February	March	April	May	June	July	August	September	October	November	December
		▨	▨	▨								
■			■	■	■							
■				▨	▨	■						
▨				▨	▨	■	■	■				
▨					▨	▨	▨	▨	▨	▨		
□					□	□						
▨						▨	▨				▨	▨
■		■	■	■	■	■	■					
■		■	■	■						■	■	
▨				▨								
■					■	■	■					
□				□	□							
										□	□	□
▨						▨	▨					
			■	■								
						■	■	■				
						▨	▨	▨				
▨							▨	▨				
						▨						
■				■	■	■						
■				■	■							
				▨	▨	▨						
						■	■	■	■			
□					□	□						
					▨	▨						
■				■	■	■						
						□	□	□	□			
				▨	▨				▨	▨		

1 ABELIA FLORIBUNDA
Mexican Abelia

U.S. zone 8

Family Caprifoliaceae.
Place of origin China.
Description A very striking shrub, rather like honeysuckle, with a round head of branches and foliage. It grows to 6–10 ft. (2–3 m.). This evergreen bears pink, delicately perfumed flowers between May and July. A highly prized plant, it is the least hardy of the *Abelia* species. Its leaves are opposite with a short stalk. This species was introduced into Europe in 1841 and the generic name derives from an English doctor, Clarke Abel, who traveled a great deal in China.
Cultivation *A. floribunda* needs protection from the wind, and good northern light (but semishade in hot climates). It requires open, well-drained, non calcareous soil with plenty of organic material. Flowering begins in the third year after planting and continues from summer to autumn. It can be grown in pots that should be sunk into the ground outdoors in the summer and brought into the shelter of a greenhouse for the winter.
Winter protection This is necessary where winters are fairly severe.
Propagation New plants can be grown by taking cuttings from the new wood in June–July.
Other species *A.* × *grandiflora*, semievergreen, with pink flowers.

2 ARUNDO DONAX
Giant Reed

U.S. zone 7

Family Gramineae.
Place of origin Mediterranean region.
Description A rhizomatous perennial between 6½–18 ft. (2–6 m.) high. Its creeping underground stem is tuberous but above ground it is about ¾ in. (2 cm). in diameter, erect, hollow and woody. The amplexicaul, lanceolate leaves are embedded in the stems, alternating at each node; they are ¾–2 in. (2–5 cm.) wide and form a sheath around the stems; their pointed tips turn back as they grow in length. The flowers are clustered into terminal panicles in the form of long, feathery brown spikes. The plant grows wild in damp, marshy places and by streams; it is often used to make fishing rods. Giant reeds are grown as windbreaks or to hide an unsightly part of the garden.
Cultivation Reeds need deep, damp soil, light and open in texture. Plant in a warm position where the clumps are protected from frost. Will need extra protection in cold districts.
Propagation This is done organically or by cutting the tips of the culms and putting them to root in sand; alternatively, they can be progagated from the rhizomes, using the parts from which the aerial culms emerge.
Other species *A. conspicua* forms very strong clumps.

3 AUCUBA JAPONICA
Japanese Aucuba

Family Cornaceae.
Place of origin Japan.
Description A bushy evergreen shrub with shiny leaves and clusters of scarlet fruit in the winter that make it very ornamental. It reaches a height of up to 13 ft. (4 m.), and branches out prolifically from the foot. Its opposite leaves are large and oval. Japanese aucuba is a dioecious plant with insignificant green and brown flowers in erect racemose inflorescences. This shrub, which is grown as an ornamental largely because of the showy, large red berries on the female plants, is sometimes sited in a group or in conjunction with the cherry laurel to create shady areas.
Cultivation This shrub adapts to any position, even in shade. It is not harmed by wind or by cold in a temperate climate. It thrives in damp, well-manured ground. Since it is dioecious, a male and one or two female plants must always be planted together in order to achieve the ornamental fruiting. Spring pruning prevents an excessive number of root suckers and helps to bring the plant into bud again.
Propagation By softwood cuttings in the summer or layering in the spring.
Other species *A. japonica* 'Maculata' has variegated leaves. *A. japonica* 'Crotonifolia' has leaves flecked with yellow. *A. japonica* 'Fructu Albo' has white fruits. *A. japonica* 'Longifolia' has long leaves.

---

4 BERBERIS VULGARIS
Common Barberry

Family Berberidaceae.
Place of origin Europe (except the north), Asia, North Africa.
Description A deciduous bushy shrub, up to 10 ft. (3 m.) high, decorative for its flowers, its little edible fruits and its beautiful autumn tints. In many areas it grows wild on hillsides and in hedgerows, in broadleaf woodlands, and pine forests. The bark of its woody branches flakes off to leave the yellow wood beneath. It is very prickly, with tripartite thorns about ¾ in. (2 cm.) long. Its small, oblong leaves are elliptic and glossy, ciliate with a serrated edge; they are darker green on the upper surface than the lower and are joined to the branches in fascicles at the thorn axils. Its small yellow flowers hang in loose racemes and smell sweetly of honey. The 6–8 petaled corolla is surrounded by 6 sepals to form a shell. The oblong, cylindrical red berries are edible but rather sour and contain 1–3 seeds; they can be used to make jams, sauces and syrups.
Cultivation The barberry should always be kept well away from any member of the Graminaceae family as it can infect it with rust. It requires a clayey, dry calcareous soil either in full sun or semishade. Pruning should be done in the spring to remove the old wood. The barberry makes an excellent pot shrub. It is hardy and very resistant to the cold.
Propagation By seed, by division of the rootsuckers or by cuttings taken in the autumn.
Other species *B. aggregata*, deciduous. *B. buxifolia* and *B. julianae*, evergreen. *B. darwinii*, evergreen with black berries. *B. thunbergii*, most widely grown species in the U.S.

5   BUDDLEJA DAVIDII
Butterfly Bush, Summer Lilac

Family   Loganiaceae.
Place of origin   China.
Description   A hardy, deciduous shrub reaching a height of 16–17 ft. (5 m.), with a straggly form. A number of sturdy growths spring up each year from the woody base and develop into slender, pendulous branches. Those of the flower-bearing year are quadrangular. The lanceolate, opposite leaves are green on the upper surface and cottony white underneath, with dentate edges. The inflorescences are borne in terminal, conical panicles, 4–12 in. (10–30 cm.) long; they spring from the leaf axils. The individual flowers have an elongated tube and a 4-lobed corolla with 4 stamens. Their colors range from deep purple through lilac, pinkish mauve, and white. The fruits consist of small, elongated capsules.

The species was named after the French missionary and naturalist, Armand David, who discovered it in Asia in the 19th century. The name of the genus derives from the English botanist, the Reverend Adam Buddle (1660–1715).

The buddleja has become naturalized in some areas. It is widely grown for its prolific summer flowers, which are attractive to butterflies.

Cultivation   The buddleja is a hardy shrub and will thrive in any kind of soil, even in an urban, polluted atmosphere, provided that it is well-drained. It needs to be sheltered from the wind which, like very heavy rain, can damage the leaves and flowers. In climates where the heat is not very great it prefers to be sited in full sun but it can withstand the cold in a mild climate. It grows well in areas ranging from coastal plains to mountain foothills and can be planted singly or in a mass to form striking splashes of color. Spring pruning should be quite drastic – even to within a foot of the ground – in order to get rid of all the previous year's growth; this prevents the plant from getting too tall and lanky and at the same time ensures larger flowers. As the flowers die during the summer the plant can be lightly pruned to encourage continuous blooming.

Winter protection   The buddleja needs protection only where the climate is very cold. Snow can break its branches.

Propagation   By seed, by stem cuttings taken in the summer or autumn from the current year's growth.

Other species   B. alternifolia, a deciduous shrub; it should not be spring pruned as its lilac-colored, scented flowers are borne on the previous year's growth. B. auriculata originates from South Africa and is suited to hot climates. Its scented creamy-white flowers appear in the winter. B. colvilei, from the Himalayas; its large, bell-shaped flowers are pink with a yellow throat; it should not be pruned. B. globosa (Orange Ball Tree), originating from Chile and Peru; its flowers are clustered together in orange spherical panicles; it is evergreen in hot countries. B. lindleyana, from China; its purple flowers have a recurved tubular calyx. B. madagascariensis, a winter-flowering shrub bearing large orange panicles. B. nivea, originating from China, with whitish pilose foliage. B. asiatica, originating from India; it bears small white, scented flowers in winter.

6 BUXUS SEMPERVIRENS
Common Box, Boxwood

U.S. zone 6

Family Buxaceae.
Place of origin Europe.
Description A hardy, evergreen shrub, sometimes arborescent in habit, growing to a height of up to 20 ft. (6 m.), with pilose branchlets that are quadrangular when young. The thick, bushy foliage consists of numerous small, oval, opposite, leathery, glossy, dark green leaves with a flattened tip; they are probably poisonous. The insignificant yellowish or light green unisexual flowers are sweetly scented and grouped in axillary clusters consisting of a central female flower surrounded by male flowers without petals. The fruit is a leathery capsule with three horns formed by the styles. Box is used as a hedge, as an edging or in bush form and grows wild in some dry, rocky areas.
Cultivation This slow-growing shrub thrives in full sun or semishade and grows in any type of soil, even when stony. It can be planted in autumn or spring and should be watered regularly until well-established. It can withstand moderate cold, wind and dryness. Pruning should be done at the end of summer to neaten hedges and keep bushes in good shape.
Propagation By softwood cuttings in the summer and hardwood cuttings in the autumn.
Other taxa *B. sempervirens* 'Aureo Variegata,' with yellow-streaked leaves. *B. sempervirens* 'Elegantissima,' with silver-marked leaves. *B. sempervirens* 'Suffruticosa,' a dwarf shrub with oval leaves, used for edgings. *B. balearica,* with paler leaves and glabrous branchlets.

---

7 CALLISTEMON SPECIOSUS
Bottlebrush

U.S. zone 9

Family Myrtaceae.
Place of origin Australia.
Description An ornamental, shrubby plant with velvety, persistent leaves; when young the branches are a reddish shade. From spring to summer it bears compact, cylindrical, scarlet floral spikes, like elegant, dainty little bottlebrushes from which the golden anthers stand out in brilliant contrast. After flowering, the branches continue to grow and clusters of terminal leaves appear above the inflorescences. *Callistemon* comes from the Greek *kalòs*, "beautiful" and *stemon*, "stamens." The brush-like appearance of the inflorescences is due to the oversized stamens in each flower.
Cultivation *Callistemon* requires a dry, very sunny position with medium to light soil; it dislikes moisture. In order to retain its ornamental qualities, it should be pruned annually in such a way that its vegetative force is equally distributed among its branches.
Propagation By seed or by cuttings taken from the mother plants and rooted in acid humus.
Other species *C. salignus,* with yellowish or slightly pink floral spikes. *C. rigidus,* with crimson flowers and very pointed linear leaves; it flowers earlier and for longer, between May and July.

8 CALLUNA VULGARIS
(syn. *Erica vulgaris*)
Heather, Ling

Family Ericaceae.
Place of origin Europe.
Description A bushy, rather dwarf, evergreen shrub, no higher than 20 in. (50 cm.), branching out prolifically into ascendant, woody branchlets. Heather is grown for the decorative value of its abundant flowers and is especially suitable for rocky gardens. Its small, glabrous, light green, opposite leaves are scale-like and grow in groups of four. The small pink flowers are arranged vertically at the tip of the branchlets to form delicately colored spikes to which bees are greatly attracted. The pendulous, campanulate corollas are enclosed within the bracts. The custom of using heather for making brooms seems to have given rise to the derivation of the name of the genus from the Greek *kalluno*, "to clean." This little shrub commonly grows wild on heath and moorland, and in mountainous regions.
Cultivation Heather grows well in soil which is siliceous, sandy, peaty, acid and poor. It withstands frost and dryness very well. The branchlets that flowered the previous year, and which retain their dry corollas throughout the winter, should be cut back in the spring.
Propagation By seed in the spring; by cuttings in the summer and autumn.
Other taxa *C. vulgaris* forma *alba*, with white flowers. *C.vulgaris* var. *hirsuta*, with pilose branchlets and leaves.
There are numerous cultivars with different characteristics: double white or pink flowers; single lilac-colored, red or white flowers; with leaves of different shades; with a fully dwarf habit.

9 CARPENTERIA CALIFORNICA
Bush Anemone, Evergreen Mock-Orange

Family Philadelphaceae.
Place of origin California.
Description Quite a large shrub that may grow to 6–15 ft. (2–4.5 m.) in height and about 6½ ft. (2 m.) across. This evergreen, with opposite leaves, is popular because of its beautiful and abundant white flowers.
Cultivation It thrives best in a mild climate. It can be planted out in good, loamy soil about April–May, when there is no danger of frost. It tolerates calcareous soil. It does not require pruning and needs only normal attention. If there are too many root suckers, they can be removed in the spring.
Winter protection If grown in an area where frosts occur, cover with burlap toward the end of autumn.
Propagation By seed in the spring in a temperate atmosphere. Softwood cuttings, with a heel, can be taken in July-August and rooted in a heated propagating frame.
Other species *C. californica* is the only species belonging to the genus *Carpenteria*.

10 CARYOPTERIS × CLANDONENSIS 'ARTHUR SIMMONDS'

U.S. zone 6

Family Verbenaceae.
Place of origin Eastern China and Japan.
Description A hybrid obtained at West Clandon in Surrey, England in 1930 by crossing *C. incana* and *C. mongolica*, both of Asiatic origin. Valued as a deciduous garden shrub, about 3 ft. (1 m.) high, for the scent of the whole plant and for the unusual dark blue of its flowers. Its green, entire, lanceolate leaves have a dentate margin. The flowers are clustered into corymbs at the leaf axils, opposite in pairs, with light-to-dark blue globose corollas from which the light blue stamens emerge. The name of the genus derives from the shape of the seeds, from the Greek meaning "winged nut."
Cultivation In a mild climate it flowers virtually throughout the summer. It grows in any type of soil – clayey or peaty, sandy or rich. It thrives in a sunny position but prefers semishade in hot areas. It reacts badly to frost but soon regenerates. It should be pruned hard in the spring to get rid of the previous year's wood and to encourage better flowering on the new season's growth.
Winter protection In areas where there may be frost, mulch the base well with humus and protect the rest of the plant with dead leaves, leafmold or straw.
Propagation By seed and by softwood cuttings.
Other species *C. incana* has gray leaves, pilose on the underside with dark blue-violet flowers gathered into thick clusters at the leaf axils. *C. mongolia*, a rather more low-growing plant with entire leaves and dark blue flowers.

---

11 CERATOSTIGMA WILLMOTTIANUM

U.S. zone 7

Family Plumbaginaceae.
Place of origin China.
Description This shrub was introduced into Europe circa 1909 from China, where it is part of the natural flora. Its name is derived from the Greek *kèrasì*, "horn" and *stigmai*, referring to the horn-like growths on the stigma; this came about because, to the Russian botanist who was studying and analysing it, the stigma seemed to be almost covered by horny appendices. It is often mistaken for the genus *Plumbago*, from which it differs only in several small characteristics. Its sky-blue flowers start to appear in July and continue until the weather begins to turn cold. They grow in terminal and axillary clusters, each flower having a large corolla and violet-colored calyx.
Cultivation It grows best in semishade where the soil is dry and light. It is suitable either for growing singly or as a colorful addition to a shrub border.
Winter protection It is able to withstand the cold fairly well but it is advisable to cover it with leaves and peat in colder areas.
Propagation By seed or by clump division. Pieces of rhizome can also be rooted but must be left undisturbed for three years before transplanting.
Other species *C. plumbaginoides*, a dwarf shrub up to 1 ft. (30 cm.), ideal for borders and shrubberies.

12 CHAMAEROPS HUMILIS
Dwarf Fan Palm, European Fan Palm

Family Palmae.

Place of origin North Africa, Europe.

Description Although this plant originates from countries with subtropical climates, where it contributes greatly to the scenery, it will thrive in mild temperate regions. In 1753 the great Swedish naturalist, Linnaeus, named this palm *Chamaerops humilis*. The Latin word *humilis*, meaning "humble" seems particularly appropriate when one compares its modest height with other palms that tower into the sky on tall, slender trunks.

This rather bushy shrub rarely reaches a height of 13 ft. (4 m.) in the wild. Its name is derived from the Greek *chamai* meaning "low on the ground."

The erect, rather squat, trunk is covered with scales left by fallen leaves, and from the tip springs a clump of broad, palmate leaves opening out like fans, each of which is divided into 10–12 long, narrow segments (laciniae). Its woody leafstalks are slim and prickly. The yellow flowers are borne in clusters of inflorescences among the clump of leaves. The fruits are reddish, fibrous, oval, inedible drupes ½–¾ in. (1–2 cm.) in length. Suckers spring from the base of the trunk and these create groups of this gregarious plant. The dwarf fan palm is widespread throughout the western Mediterranean area of Europe and North Africa where it infiltrates into the rocky, stony, arid scrublands (*maquis*) and coastal regions. This plant has been known since antiquity, when its leaves and fibers had many uses.

Cultivation It is suitable for planting in a large pot or in the open. It withstands low temperatures for short periods but is able to survive in hot, dry climates.

Winter protection It can stand a little frost if the winter is not exceptionally hard, but it may require some form of protection.

Propagation By seed or suckers.

13 CHIMONANTHUS PRAECOX
(syn. *C. fragrans, Calycanthus praecox*)
Winter Sweet   **U.S. zone 5**

Family Calycanthaceae.
Place of origin China.
Description This erect deciduous shrub is many-branched
and may reach a height of 10 ft. (3 m.). It is grown mainly for its
scented flowers, which appear on the bare branches in winter,
hence the name of the genus from the Greek *cheimon*, "winter"
and *anthos*, "flower." Its large, lanceolate, opposite leaves are
rugose; they are green but darker on the upper surface than the
lower; their margin is entire and they are about 4 in. (10 cm.)
long. The strongly scented flowers are star-shaped and yellow
with a reddish center. Its fruits are long, brown drupes and rather
large, each with a single seed.
Cultivation Winter sweet is extremely hardy and withstands
the cold well. It is slow-growing and thrives in a sunny position in
well-drained, clayey soil enriched with humus or leafmold.
Requires regular watering because it cannot stand dryness.
Propagation By seed in the autumn, by air layering, by shoot
layering in the autumn.
Other taxa *C. praecox* 'Grandiflorus,' with large, less scented
flowers.

---

14 CHOISYA TERNATA
Mexican Orange Flower   **U.S. zone 7**

Family Rutaceae.
Description A charming evergreen shrub with dazzling,
scented flowers, it grows to a height of 10 ft. (3 m.). Its long,
green, often trifoliate leaves are glossy and elliptic. Its white,
sweet-smelling flowers each have 5 petals with a prominent little
clump of yellow stamens in the center.
Cultivation It grows well in a mild climate, not too dry or too
hot, in damp, non calcareous soil, well broken down with humus,
leafmold or even sand. It needs plentiful watering during the
summer or in dry periods. In areas where the climate is less
favorable it can be grown against a wall. It can also be cultivated
in a pot. It thrives outdoors in a sunny position or even in
semishade. It lends itself well to rocky gardens or to forming
isolated clumps of color. It does not like being transplanted.
Winter protection This is necessary if the cold is very intense
and prolonged.
Propagation By cuttings in the summer.

15 CHRYSANTHEMUM FRUTESCENS
French Marguerite   **U.S. zone 8**

Family Compositae.
Place of origin Canary Islands.
Description An evergreen perennial of up to 5 ft. (1.5 m.) in height, it is grown as an ornamental plant both indoors and in the garden. Its green, deeply lobed leaves are grayish on the lower surface. The flowers are single and have the classic daisy form on erect, rigid stems. The name of the genus derives from the Greek *chrysos*, "gold" and *anthos*, "flower," because of the brilliant golden disk in the center of each flower which gives the bush a very showy appearance.
Cultivation Chrysanthemums need soil that is well-drained, well-manured and loamy, with constant moisture. The young plants can be planted out in May, each with its own stake, in a position that is sheltered from the wind and excessive heat. They also grow well in pots. The tops should be pinched out in June and regular disbudding carried out throughout the summer months. The selective removal of side shoots will reduce the number of flowers, ensuring early flowering and larger flowers. Do not allow to dry out.
Winter protection This chrysanthemum cannot withstand frost and should either be protected or put under cover.
Propagation By seed, by cuttings of the basal shoots in the autumn.

---

16 CISTUS CRETICUS
Rock Rose   **U.S. zone 7**

Family Cistaceae.
Place of origin Mediterranean regions.
Description A variable evergreen shrub, it grows to a height of about 3 ft. (1 m.) in its native coastal and inland areas. Its branchlets are erect and crowded. The short-stemmed leaves are oval and elliptic, ¾–2¾ in. (2–7 cm.) long; they are green and wrinkled on the upper surface, grayish and softly pilose underneath, with a crinkly margin. The purplish pink flowers, with their short yellow stamens, are arranged in vertical groups; each has 5 crinkly petals which are yellow at the base. The capsules are pilose and round. Several different taxa of rock rose are often grown together for their decorative clumps of color.
Cultivation Rock roses require siliceous, dry soil and should be sited in a hot, sunny position in mild to hot climates. The old wood can be cut out in the spring. It is not a long-lived plant but it throws up new growth from the base.
Propagation Reproduction by seed is not always true and it is better to take cuttings in the summer.
Other species *C. crispus* with pink flowers, crinkly leaves, and downy branches. *C. ladanifer* with large white flowers and violet blotches at the base of each petal. *C. laurifolius*, the most resistant to cold, has white flowers with yellow blotches at the base of the petals. *C. monspeliensis* has leaves that are inrolled at the margins and white flowers. *C. salvifolius*, with white, often solitary, flowers.

Family Verbenaceae.

Place of origin China and Japan.

Description A sturdy, deciduous shrub, reaching a height of 10–20 ft. (3–6 m.), with expansive growth. With its spreading branches and single, rugose trunk, it sometimes looks more like a small tree. The opposite, ovate to elliptic, subcordate leaves are 4–8 in. (10–20 cm.) long; their upper surface is dark green and the lower pale gray. Its numerous little scented white flowers are grouped in cymes, each flower having a red campanulate calyx with an open tubular 5-lobed corolla.

Its fruits are quite spectacular, consisting of a dark blue berry supported by 5 bright red calyx lobes. This plant is grown for the decorative quality of its sweetly scented flowers and for its brightly colored fruits, which stay on the plant throughout the winter.

Cultivation *Clerodendron* requires a warm and sheltered position in semishade, because, although reasonably hardy, it cannot withstand frost very well. It thrives even in sandy soil, provided this is loamy and well-drained. It becomes thicker and more shrublike as its numerous suckers develop into new plants. The tangle of branches can be opened up by pruning in spring when any branches killed by frost should also be removed; the pruning can be quite hard if there is a lot of damage.

Winter protection In cold areas these plants should be sheltered by a wall.

Propagation New plants can be grown from the root shoots by division of the clump in the spring and of the suckers in the autumn. Cuttings can be taken in the summer or seed sown in the spring. Transplanting is done in October or March.

Other species *C. bungei*, a deciduous, hardy shrub with downy branches, originates from China; it blooms profusely in a rotund mass of scented pink flowers; it needs to be sited in full sun since it dies back if frostbitten but quickly regenerates; propagation is by division of the root ramifications. *C. trichotomum* var. *fargesii*, a native of China, very hardy. Leaves purple-red when young becoming glossy green later; they have an unpleasant odor when crushed. The calyces are green, and the flowers white and scented. *C. myricoides* from Africa has lavender-blue flowers and cannot withstand the cold. *C. thomsoniae*; this evergreen climber from West Africa should be grown in a pot indoors; it needs semishade and a great deal of water; in the spring it produces pendulous flowers with a white calyx, a red corolla, and long white stamens.

18 COLUTEA ARBORESCENS
Bladder Senna

U.S. zone 6

Family Leguminosae.

Place of origin Eastern Europe and the Mediterranean.

Description A thornless deciduous shrub of erect, bushy habit reaching a height of 10–20 ft. (3–6 m.) when cultivated. Its pale green leaves are alternate and imparipinnate with 7–15 elliptic to obovate leaflets, glabrous on the upper surface, and slightly downy on the underside. The papilionaceous flowers, 3/4 in. (2 cm.) long, are grouped in small, erect racemes; each flower has a pilose calyx and a yellow corolla of which the larger, upright petal (vexillum) has brown markings. The fruit is a pendulous, membranous, dilated pod about 2⅜–2¾ in. (6–7 cm.) long; if this bladder-shaped seed vessel is squeezed between the fingers before it is ripe, it will burst with a sharp report. When ripe, the pod becomes dehiscent, parchment-like and reddish; out of it come 20–30 seeds that can be poisonous to some people.

Cultivation It requires heat in the summer and cannot withstand very low temperatures in the winter. It thrives in full sun where the soil is calcareous and clayey, even stony. Bladder senna is grown for its long-lasting clusters of flowers and the striking quality of its ornamental fruits. It is a hardy plant, apart from its intolerance of frost. It can be pruned hard in the spring.

Propagation By seed in the spring or natural dispersal in July, by hardwood cuttings in the autumn. It can be transplanted, with a good rootball, from November to March.

Other species *C. orientalis* is similar to *C. arborescens* but is not grown as much. Its flowers are brownish red or copper.

---

19 CORYLOPSIS SPICATA

U.S. zone 6

Family Hamamelidaceae.

Place of origin Japan.

Description A deciduous shrub, rather similar to the hazel in appearance and habit, as its name, which derives from the Greek, implies (*korylos*, "hazel nut," and *opsis*, "like"). It has a bushy, spreading habit with flexible branchlets and light green foliage; it grows to a maximum height of 6½ ft. (2 m.). Its light green leaves are cordate. The flowers emerge on the branches before the leaves, in early spring; the small yellow corollas are grouped in long, pendulous, scented spikes. The black, round seeds are contained in the fruit, which is top-shaped.

Cultivation The delicate coloring of the foliage and early, sweet-smelling flowers are this shrub's most attractive features. It is not very hardy even in a temperate climate, and in cold areas must be sheltered from frost and wind; it should be sited in a sunny position where the tender early buds will not be damaged. It requires a loose, well-manured soil. No pruning needed.

Winter protection In climates where spring frosts are possible protect with plastic sheeting or burlap.

Propagation By seed in the spring, by cuttings in the summer or, better still, by layering started in October. Transplant, into loamy, peaty soil between October and March.

Other species *C. glabrescens*, originating from Japan, is hardy, with obovate leaves and scented, pale yellow flowers. *C. pauciflora* has yellow flowers. *C. willmottiae*, the loveliest of the species, which has long, dense flowering clusters with prickly stems; it has difficulty in withstanding cold springs.

20 CORNUS SANGUINEA
Red Dogwood, Common Dogwood

U.S. zone 4

Family Cornaceae.

Place of origin Europe.

Description This deciduous shrub is commonly found in broadleaf woods, copses, hedgerows and wasteland, where it provides food and shelter for birds. It grows to a height of 13 ft. (4 m.) and has slender, flexible branchlets with a reddish bark that becomes blood-red in the winter, hence the Latin specific name, *sanguinea*, meaning "blood color." The branches were, at one time, used for making wickerwork and toothpicks.

Its opposite, ovate leaves are broad; their upper surface is glabrous and the lower pubescent; they turn red in the autumn. Its little white flowers have a 4-petaled corolla without bracts and are clustered into numerous cymes at the end of the branches. It first blooms in the late spring and sometimes a second time in the autumn. Its inedible fruits are small, globose, bitter-tasting drupes; they turn from green to a blackish blue with tiny white spots. An oil can be extracted from their seeds. The wood is hard and can be used to make baskets and trellises etc.

Cultivation It prefers a clayey or calcareous soil but also grows in stony or sandy ground. It thrives in either a sunny or semishaded position but the branchlets redden better in the former. In the wild it is often found growing in groups to form clumps of bushes. When cultivated as a single plant, this colonizing habit makes it particularly suitable for planting on sloping ground where the soil is prone to erosion, as its numerous roots and suckers hold the soil together well. They are, however, invasive.

Propagation By using the stolons, suckers, seeds and by cuttings.

Other species To grow as ground cover or for rock gardens: *C. canadensis*, a quick-spreading herbaceous perennial. Grows equally well in sun or shade; produces greenish-purple flowers in June and round, red fruits. Prefers damp, acid soil and can be increased by division.

Ornamental species to grow for their decorative foliage: *C. alba*, a deciduous bush originating from Siberia, it has white fruits and red leaves and twigs in the autumn. Grows well in clayey, very damp soil. *C. stolonifera*, (Red Osier Dogwood), like all the blood-red stemmed plants it should be pruned right back to the base in early spring to encourage new branchlets that will change color in the autumn. Likes a sunny or semishaded position.

Species to grow for their ornamental bracts: *C. capitata* (Bentham's Cornel), a large evergreen shrub originating from the Himalayas and China, it has yellow bracts and plump edible red fruits. Cannot withstand frost. *C. kousa* (Japanese or Korean Dogwood); see separate entries.

CORYLUS AVELLANA
Hazel, Cobnut

Family Betulaceae.

Place of origin Europe, western Asia, North Africa.

Description A shrub, 13–20 ft. (4–6 m.) high, with numerous suckers springing from a single bole base giving it a bushy shape; all the branches grow straight up from the base and have thick deciduous foliage. The bark is brown and blotchy on young wood and then flakes off; the young twigs are pilose and hispid. The alternate leaves are obovate-cordate at the base, 2–4¾ in. (5–12 cm.) long, with hairy stalks; they have doubly-dentate margins and are hairy and dark green on the upper surface, velvety and a lighter shade on the lower, with an acuminate tip. This is a monoecious plant with unisexual masculine flowers in the form of pendulous catkins ¾–3⅛ in. (2–8 cm.) long; these appear in the autumn and become yellow as winter progresses; the insignificant female flowers are greenish buds with red styles and stigmas that appear in the winter. The fruit is a globose, pointed nut protected by campanulate, laciniate bracts that are open at the top and fleshy at the base; these become dehiscent when ripe. The shape acounts for the derivation of the name of the genus, which comes from the Greek *korys*, meaning "helmet."

Hazelnuts grow either singly or in clusters and fall when ripe. This shrub grows wild in woods, copses and in damp lowlands up to an elevation of about 4,600 ft. (1,400 m.). Its early flowering makes the hazel very attractive to bees in early spring. The hazel has been widely used as a pioneer plant to re-establish the balance of a broadleaf forest or to establish a new one. It has been cultivated since antiquity for its delightful edible fruits, which also provide food for rodents and birds.

Cultivation The hazel seeks the light and prefers loamy soil. When transplanting this shrub, give it well-worked and manured soil with a good, reasonably moist tilth; afterwards, a dressing of humus every year will produce good results. It can be sited in a sunny or windy position since it is not self-fertilizing and relies on the wind for cross-fertilization. For this reason several plants should be grouped close together to permit wind-pollination and thus ensure a good crop of nuts. New bushes can be planted between spring or autumn at a distance of 10–17 ft. (3–5 m.) from each other. When the plants are well-developed, they should be pruned at the end of every winter to keep them young and increase their fruiting potential by eliminating any young sterile shoots.

Propagation By transplanting the suckers, by air layering, by simple layering in the autumn, and by grafting. If an old plant no longer bears fruit, it can be rejuvenated by cutting it back to its base.

Other taxa Ornamental cultivars: *C.avellana* 'Aurea,' with yellow leaves, *C.avellana* 'Contorta' (Corkscrew Hazel, Harry Lauder's Walking Stick), with branches that twist into a spiral. *C. maxima*, originating from the Balkans, with large fruit enclosed in a flask-shaped cupule growing singly or in groups of 2–3. *C. maxima* 'Purpurea,' with reddish leaves and purple catkins.

22 COTINUS COGGYGRIA
(syn. *Rhus cotinus*)
Smoke Bush, Venetian Sumach

U.S. zone 6

Family Anacardiaceae.
Place of origin Eastern and Mediterranean Europe.
Description A deciduous shrub with prolific foliage that shades into brilliant autumnal colors to provide a spectacular display. In the wild, the smoke bush grows in hilly and mountainous areas of the Mediterranean and in subalpine regions in any type of soil, although mainly calcareous. This plant, which grows to a height of 10 ft. (3 m.), has a bushy habit and a resinous smell. Its ovate, rounded, alternate, green leaves are 1½–2¾ in. (4–7 cm.) in length, smooth, with a long stalk and prominent venation; their lower surface is lead-colored; at the end of the summer the leaves take on wonderful shades of gold, red and violet. The rather insignificant little pink flowers, which are mostly sterile, are grouped into large, loose, drooping panicles. The few fertile flowers produce small, reddish-brown drupes, distributed among the numerous hairy stalks of the sterile flowers. The whole bush has a smoky appearance that well justifies its being called the smoke bush.
Cultivation It likes a warm position and dry soil rich in mineral salts. The young plants need moist peat or organic compost, shelter from cold winds, and watering in the spring.
Winter protection The young plants should be protected from frost.
Propagation By seed, by cuttings in the summer, by division of the suckers, or by simple layering of the more flexible branches in September.

23 COTONEASTER HORIZONTALIS
U.S. zone 5

Family Rosaceae.
Place of origin China.
Description A low-growing, horizontally spreading shrub with prostrate branchlets that open out like a fan and branch off in herringbone fashion over the ground. Its tiny, glossy, dark green leaves are ovate, leathery and semipersistent. Its little pink flowers are bell-like and appear singly or in groups in the leaf axils. The brilliant scarlet fruits are small and round with a diameter of ¼ in. (0.5 cm.). This shrub can be grown as ground cover to choke weeds and to blanket anything at ground level. It is particularly decorative in the autumn when it is covered with red drupes and forms a delightful patch of red autumn color in rock gardens and over low walls and banks.
Cultivation It is hardy and resistant to the cold; does not need much looking after but has a tendency to be invasive. It can be cut back, when necessary, to keep it tidy.
Propagation By seed, by simple layering, or by softwood cuttings taken with a heel in July to August.
Other species Dwarf species to use as ground cover are: *C. adpressus*, originating from China, a creeping, hardy shrub with tiny flowers and small red fruits; it even tolerates a polluted city atmosphere. *C. dammeri*, a low-growing evergreen shrub for cold, shady areas. *C. lacteus*, an evergreen with clusters of red autumn fruits, ideal for creating thick hedges; its creamy-white flowers appearing in June–July. *C. microphyllus*, of Himalayan and Chinese origin.

24 CRATAEGUS OXYACANTHA
Hawthorn, May, Whitethorn

Family Rosaceae.

Place of origin Europe, including the British Isles.

Description A long-lived deciduous shrub that grows to a height of 20 ft. (6 m.), it has a straggly crown and is very thorny. Its lobed leaves are leathery and its little 5-petaled flowers are white, sometimes pink, and clustered into corymbs. The fruit consists of a red, fleshy drupe, round, with a depression at the apex with a small corona and up to ⅜ in. (1 cm.) in diameter; it contains 2–3 seeds. Its roots are very deep and find sufficient water in the subsoil to keep the plant nourished. The dark gray bark is inclined to split as time passes.

Its fruits were highly prized by the European prehistoric palafittic lake-dwellers who used them, dried or ground, in place of cereals. Today some parts of the plant are used therapeutically. Under cultivation, it is used to make protective hedges and grows to about 6½ ft. (2 m.) in 6 years. It is also used to prevent erosion. It is a favorite with birds both as a nesting site and for its fruits. Numerous species of hawthorn grow wild in Europe, western Asia, North Africa and North America. The generic name comes from the Greek *kratos*, meaning "strength," a reference to the strong and durable wood.

Cultivation To create a hedge, a trench about 20 in. (50 cm.) wide and the same depth should be dug a few months before planting, which is best carried out in the spring or autumn. All straggly growth can be cut back every winter.

Propagation By seed, by grafting and, more commonly, by transplanting.

Other taxa The following are grown for their decorative value: *C. oxyacantha* forma *aurea*, yellow fruit, 'Plena,' double white flowers, 'Punicea,' single red flowers, 'Rosea,' single pink, scented flowers. *C. azarolus*, (Azarole), with large, edible fruit, ¾ in. (2 cm.) in diameter, a long-lived plant up to 33 ft. (10 m.) high. *C. crus-galli*, (Cockspur Thorn), a small tree with prominent spines originating from North America, sometimes used as stock for fruit trees, its leaves turning scarlet in the autumn. *C. laciniata*, a native of the Orient, it has orange fruits. *C. monogyna* is unique in having a single style; it is very attractive to birds and can be used to make hedges. *C. pentagyna* grows wild in central-eastern Europe; it has blackish fruits with 5 seeds. *C. prunifolia*, a tall, spiny North American shrub or small tree growing to a height of up to 20 ft. (6 m.).

25 CHAENOMELES SPECIOSA
Flowering Quince

Family Rosaceae.

Place of origin Japan.

Description A bushy deciduous shrub with strongly ascendant, spiny branches and a broad, expansive head. As a cultivated plant it can be grown either as a dense shrub with interwoven branches or trained along a wall. It is slow-growing and reaches a height of about 6½ ft. (2 m.). Its smooth, leathery ovate leaves are glossy and about 1⅛–2 in. (3–5 cm.) long. Its scarlet-crimson flowers, have 5 petals, are about 1⅛ in. (3 cm.) across and grouped in clusters. The freely produced flowers appear before the leaves. Its fruits are like small, round apples, green at first, then shading to gold as they ripen; they have an aromatic scent and are sometimes used to perfume rooms and cupboards; they are edible when cooked and can be used to make jelly, jam and liqueurs. The flowering quince is a very decorative plant and can be grown singly, as a hedge or against a wall or balustrade, where its brilliant flowers make an attractive springtime display.

Cultivation It is a hardy plant and easy to grow. It thrives in any type of soil and in any position, even against a north-facing wall. Neither frost nor a polluted atmosphere harms it, but it likes a certain amount of moisture. To keep it in shape, it can be trimmed in early summer, after flowering, since the flowers are borne on the previous year's growth. When an ornamental quince is trained as an espalier or against a wall, the lateral branches should not be pruned so harshly as to discourage the naturally exuberant and very decorative growth. Young plants can be planted in spring or autumn. In a hedge they should be placed at intervals of 3 ft. (90 cm.). The flowering branches last well in water and make an attractive indoor decoration; they should be cut just before the buds open.

Propagation By branch or root cuttings in the autumn, by simple layering, by seed, or by division of the root suckers.

Other taxa *C. japonica* 'Alpina,' a fine shrub with brilliant red flowers. *C. speciosa* 'Moerloosii,' with pink and white flowers. *C. speciosa* 'Nivalis,' with white flowers. *C. speciosa* 'Simonii,' with red semidouble flowers. *C. × superba* 'Rowallane,' suitable for hedges, with bright red flowers. *C. cathayensis*, originating from China, with white flowers and oval fruits, is hardy.

26 CYTISUS SCOPARIUS
Common Broom

Family Leguminosae.
Place of origin Western Europe, including the British Isles.
Description A deciduous shrub with long, slender branches which become tangled and bushy as they grow upward. Its small, trifoliate leaves fall early, leaving the branches bare. The papilionaceous flowers are ¾ in. (2 cm.) long, growing singly at intervals along the branches at the leaf axils; its fruits turn black when ripe. This plant is grown for its abundant flowers and long flowering period; it is suitable for rock gardens or for growing in clumps or rows.
Cultivation This is an undemanding plant; as it is able to thrive by itself, as long as it is in a sunny, warm position. It grows in dry soil, even when loose and sandy, and enriches the soil with nitrogen. It should be pruned every year to prevent it from becoming too tall and straggly; the pruning can start as flowering ends in June or July. Cut back to where the new shoots are forming.
Propagation By seed in the spring, by cuttings in the summer.
Other taxa *C. scoprarius* 'Andreanus,' with reddish wing petals. *D. battandieri*, with aromatic yellow flowers for a sunny position. *C. × beanii*, with yellow flowers; a ground cover for rock gardens. *C. × dallimorei*, with pink flowers. *C. grandiflorus*, with larger flowers and pilose fruits. *C. multiflorus*, with numerous small white flowers. *C. × praecox*, with clusters of unpleasantly scented yellow flowers. *C. purpureus*, with pink flowers.

---

27 DATURA STRAMONIUM
Thorn Apple

Family Solanaceae.
Place of origin North America.
Description A herbaceous annual about 1–2 ft. (30–60 cm.) tall with dense branches and leaves. The stem is erect, robust and dichotomous. The large, ovate leaves are acuminate and slightly dentate with long stems. The flowers, which grow singly, are erect, white or occasionally purple, and about 4 in. (10 cm.) long. The tubiform corolla emerges from the pentagonal calyx and opens into 5 narrowly acuminate lobes. Its fruit consists of an erect capsule with short prickles, about the size of a walnut, containing black, kidney-shaped seeds in its valves. The thorn apple grows wild on wasteland, among ruins and in hedgerows and is widely naturalized throughout the temperate and subtropical parts of the northern hemisphere. It is believed to have been dispersed widely by gypsies who used it as an empirical medicine. As a result, it was known in the Middle Ages as "the devil's herb" or "witches' herb."
Cultivation It thrives best in a clayey, calcareous, rich soil in a warm to hot climate but in a position that is not too dry. The thorn apple is deadly poisonous and must not be eaten. It is not recommended for the garden.
Propagation By seed sown in April.
Other species *D. ferox*, originating from southern Europe, with small bluish-white flowers and prickly fruit; *D. metel*, a hairy plant with strongly scented white flowers about 8 in. (20 cm.) long and rather broad, which are followed by prickly, pendulous fruit.

DEADLY POISONOUS

28 DAPHNE MEZEREUM
Mezereon

Family Thymeleaceae.
Place of origin Europe and Siberia.
Description A deciduous shrub with a bushy habit and erect, flexible stems springing from the base, up to 3¼ ft. (1 m.) in height. Its small pink, tubiform, strongly scented flowers have a long calyx that opens into 4 horizontal petals; they are grouped in clusters along the stems and are in bloom before the leaves appear. These are light green, soft and smooth, lanceolate and arranged in terminal rosettes. The fruit is a round berry about the size of a pea and changes from green to a shiny red as it ripens; it is poisonous.

Mezereon grows wild in copses and conifer woods as well as in pastures up to an elevation of about 6,562 ft. (2,000 m.). It is cultivated for the very decorative, showy quality of its early bloom, and is useful in rock gardens and to fill a shady corner.

Cultivation This daphne needs open, light soil, preferably calcareous, peaty and even a little clayey. It likes a sunny or semishaded position, sheltered from the wind. It needs to be kept moist and requires regular watering during the heat of summer, especially if in a sunny position. It is a hardy plant and can withstand frost. Spring pruning should be done only to remove any dead or crossed branches. Young plants can be transplanted in spring or autumn and should be well-mulched with peat and leafmold.

Propagation The fruits can be put in the ground in early summer or in the autumn. Cuttings can be taken in the summer or air layering carried out in the spring.

Other taxa *D. mezereum* forma *alba* has white flowers. *D. mezereum* 'Grandiflora' has large, purple flowers. *D. mezereum* 'Alba Plena' has double white flowers. *D. alpina* has scented white flowers arranged in terminal clusters, pilose leaves and yellowish-red fruit. *D. blagayana*, an evergreen bush with creamy white flowers in April and May, suitable for rock gardens in a temperate climate. *D. cneorum*, an evergreen bushy shrub with strongly scented, showy pink flowers in the late spring followed by yellow berries; suitable for rock gardens on non calcareous soil. *D. collina*, an evergreen shrub with slightly scented pink flowers, suitable for shrub borders. *D. laureola*, an evergreen shrub with greenish flowers and black fruits; *D. striata*, a dwarf evergreen shrub with scented pink flowers, suitable for gardens in mountainous regions. *D.* × *burkwoodii* has pink and then white flowers, strongly scented, grouped into dense terminal clusters; its leaves are semievergreen and it has red berries.

29 DEUTZIA SCABRA
(syn. *D. crenata*)

Family   Philadelphaceae.

Place of origin   Japan and China.

Description   This deutzia is a very popular shrub because of its fine show of flowers in June. Its name derives from that of the Dutch naturalist Johann van der Deutz, the distinguished friend and patron of the Swedish discoverer of the genus Carl Peter Thunberg.

This deciduous shrub is sometimes quite small but can grow to 10 ft. (3 m.) in height. Its very ornamental leaves are opposite, dentate-serrate and rugose with prominent venation. The white or pink flowers are arranged in clusters, each with a 5-petaled or double corolla. Pride of Rochester is an especially popular variety of *D. scabra*. The wood is highly prized although its use is restricted because the trunk, being that of a shrub, is quite small; in Japan it is sought after for intarsia work (mosaic woodwork) and for making wooden nails.

Cultivation   Easy to grow, this plant can be used for hedging or as a bush; it adapts to any type of soil and position but cannot tolerate dryness. It can survive even in a polluted city atmosphere. It begins to bloom when very young; if the flowers are sparse, it may be due to lack of light, lack of nourishment or lack of water. It should be pruned in the summer, when the flowering season ends, to prevent the bush becoming too dense. A dressing of manure in late spring is beneficial.

Winter protection   If the plant is in a very cold position it can be protected with straw or plastic.

Propagation   Cuttings root very easily and can be transplanted in spring or autumn into good, loamy soil.

Other species   *D. gracilis*, with panicles of white flowers, is used to make hedges. *D. longifolia*, with lilac-colored flowers. *D. vilmoriniae*, with broad white flowerheads.

Family Elaeagnaceae.

Place of origin Japan.

Description A sweetly scented evergreen shrub mainly grown for its decorative winter foliage. It is used to cover walls or form hedges or clumps, and is suitable for seaside gardens. It is a prickly plant with leathery, elliptic leaves and undulate margins; green on the upper surface and silvery white on the lower. In the spring groups of little white flowers appear in the leaf axils. The name of the genus possibly derives from the Greek *elaia*, meaning "olive tree," a probable reference to the shape and color of the leaves, which resemble those of the olive.

Cultivation *Elaeagnus* requires a deep, loamy soil; it withstands the cold well and adapts equally well to city and seaside climates where, particularly in the latter case, it is used as a windbreak. It benefits from a dressing of manure every spring and young plants need plenty of water. When used as a hedge, the plants should be spaced at 16 in. (40 cm.) intervals. Plant in spring or autumn. If the hedge becomes too thick or if growth is too vigorous, the shrubs can be pruned hard in the spring.

Propagation By cuttings or seed in August. Transplanting can be done in April but the young plants should be sheltered from the wind.

Other species The genus includes some hardier deciduous species and evergreens that are grown for their ornamental effect. Other species are better known for their fruits and are cultivated for them in Asia. Among the more important are: *E. × ebbingei*, a hybrid of *E. macrophylla* and *E. pungens*; a quick-growing evergreen shrub with ovate, leathery, silvery-gray leaves; its white flowers are followed by small red or orange oval fruits; very suitable for hedges and windbreaks, especially near the sea. It is one of the more resistant evergreen shrubs with delicately scented flowers; it should be sited in the sun or slight shade and withstands the cold well.

Family Ericaceae.
Place of origin Japan.
Description A deciduous shrub growing 12–15 ft. (3–5 m.) with brilliant autumn shades of yellow-red. The name of the genus means a "pregnant flower." In May its inflorescences appear in umbelliferous terminal racemes; the flowers are orange-yellow veined with red, and the corollas are campanulate, hence the specific name. The leaves are dentate, aristate and pilose.
Cultivation The most important features of *Enkianthus* are its attractive leaves, especially in autumn, and its pretty flowers. It is slow-growing. The most important element to ensure that it thrives is the soil, which should be predominantly an acid peat. It likes damp ground and therefore requires frequent watering in the summer. Little pruning is necessary except to remove dead and unnecessary wood.
Propagation By cuttings, even though transplanting is difficult owing to the length of time the roots take to form; cuttings should be taken from two- to three-year-old wood and potted up to root in a cold greenhouse.
Other species *E. perulatus*, a Japanese species with white flowers and magnificent autumn color. *E. chinensis*, with yellowish flowers edged with red.

---

32 ERICA ARBOREA
Tree Heath

U.S. zone 6

Family Ericaceae.
Place of origin Southern Europe, North Africa, and parts of eastern and central Africa, northern Asia Minor.
Description An erect, compact evergreen shrub, 3–20 ft. (1–6 m.) high, slow growing. Widespread in the Mediterranean regions, where it is found on high slopes and in groves of cork oaks, chestnuts and holmoak together with rock roses, arbutus and broom. Its young branches are pilose and the leaves hairless, linear and in whorls of 3–4. Its sweetly scented flowers consist of small white or pink corollas closely arranged along pendulous terminal spikes. It is a favorite plant of bees. The tree heath was at one time used to make brooms and is still used sometimes for garden besoms. The butt of the trunk is also used occasionally to make briar pipes.
Cultivation It thrives in acid, dry, siliceous soil and hates lime. It prefers a shady position in hotter areas. The dead flowers and old, straggly branches should be trimmed off in the spring.
Propagation By seed, by layering, by cuttings from the current year's shoots in August. Transplanting can be done in spring or autumn.
Other species *E. herbacea*, with deep pink, white or red flowers, likes dry, calcareous, humus-rich soil. *E. cinerea* (Bell Heather), with violet-colored flowers. *E. multiflora*, with pink corollas. *E. scoparia*, a mainly Mediterranean species with small, greenish flowers. *E. terminalis*, 9 ft. (3 m.) with pink corollas gathered in terminal spikes. *E. tetralix*, (Cross-Leaved Heath), with pink flowers, prefers damp, acid soil.

33 EXOCHORDA KOROLKOWII
(syn. *E. albertii*)

U.S. zone 6

Family Rosaceae.

Place of origin Turkestan.

Description *Exochorda* is a very beautiful but little-known genus of which there are only four species. It is a deciduous shrub with alternate, oblong, petiolate leaves. In May its white flowers are borne in erect racemes. The height of this shrub varies between 6½ and 13 ft. (2–4 m.).

Cultivation *Exochorda* is easy to grow. It needs good, deep, loamy soil and adapts very well to all climates, preferring a sunny, open position. Pruning can be done every two or three years, when the oldest branches should be cut out to leave only the younger, stronger growth.

Propagation By seed outdoors in the spring, or by softwood cuttings during the summer.

Other species *E. racemosa* (*E. grandiflora*), 10 ft. (3¼ m.) high, is the most beautiful of the species, very compact and rounded; it is covered with large, white, 5-petaled flowers in May. *E. giraldii*, originating from China.

34 FATSIA JAPONICA
(syn. *Aralia japonica*)

U.S. zone 7

Family Araliaceae.

Place of origin Japan.

Description Fatsia is the Latinized version of the Japanese name for this plant. The leaves of Fatsia are lobate-palmate, evergreen and glossy, creating a very ornamental effect. Around August it produces globose clusters of creamy-white flowers in pyramidal inflorescences that last until October. These are followed by groups of large, black fruits that are used as dyes.

Cultivation A half-hardy plant, it thrives outdoors in temperate climates. It can be transplanted between April and May and needs frequent watering in dry, hot weather. No regular pruning is necessary.

Winter protection In very cold winters, it should be potted up and kept in a greenhouse or indoors; if it is growing outside, against a wall, it can be protected by covering its base with leaves or straw.

Propagation By well-ripened seeds sown under glass or by cuttings rooted in sand.

Other species A related plant that used to be put in the genus *Fatsia* is *Tetrapanax papyriferus* (Rice-Paper Plant), once known as *F. papyrifera*. This is widely used in the Far East to make rice paper and artist's paper for painting. It is a native of Taiwan and mainland China and grows to a height of 16–20 ft. (5–6 m.) in its native habitat. This is tender and needs conservatory treatment in the British Isles.

35 FORSYTHIA SUSPENSA
Golden Bell

Family Oleaceae.
Place of origin China.
Description A deciduous shrub up to 6½ ft. (2 m.), branching out vigorously from the base. It is grown for the showiness of its early flowering and for its graceful, elegant habit. Its lanceolate, ovate leaves, which appear after the flowers, are about 4 in. (10 cm.) long, sometimes trifoliate, and with finely serrate margins. The golden-yellow flowers, which are borne along the branches either singly or in groups of 3, are tubular at the base opening out into 4 long petals. The genus is named after the 18th-century British horticulturalist William Forsyth.
Cultivation This plant grows in any soil. Pruning should be carried out immediately after flowering but should not be so drastic that the shape of the shrub is changed. A sunny position, especially in areas where the weather is cold, encourages the most prolific production of flowers. *Forsythia* is also suitable for shady areas but does not bloom as well. It is very hardy and withstands frosts but does not tolerate dryness. It is equally decorative when grown singly, against a wall, in shrubberies or as a hedge; in the latter case there should be a space of 24 in. (60 cm.) between plants.
Propagation By layering, by autumn cuttings.
Other taxa *F. suspensa* var. *sieboldii* has long hanging branches and yellow flowers tinged with red. *F. suspensa* 'Pallida' has pale yellow flowers. *F. viridissima* has clusters of numerous yellow flowers. *F. × intermedia* has erect and hanging branches; it flowers prolifically.

---

36 FUCHSIA MAGELLANICA

Family Onagraceae.
Place of origin Chile, Argentina.
Description A deciduous bushy shrub with opposite leaves and weeping branches. It reaches a height of about 12 ft. (4 m.). The calyces of its pendulous flowers open up into 4 divaricate red lobes to surround the long, closed purple petals from which the stylus and stamens emerge. The fruits are black berries.
Cultivation This plant is able to withstand the cold well in a mild climate and comes back into growth quite easily. It is not difficult to grow. It needs to be sited in semishade or in full sun if the climate is not excessively hot. It likes deep, loamy soil and needs to be kept well-watered. Fuchsias grow well in pots in a good mixture of loam and humus. All frost-damaged branches can be cut back hard in the spring. During the summer the plants should be deadheaded regularly to prolong flowering.
Winter protection In a cold climate the plants should ideally be sheltered in a greenhouse or indoors. If left outside, the bases should be well-mulched with weathered ashes, peat or leaves.
Propagation By cuttings in summer or by division of the root suckers in autumn or spring.
Other taxa *F. magellanica* 'Riccartonii' forms a dense hedge. *F. corymbiflora*, from South America, has pendulous clusters of flowers. *F. microphylla*, from Mexico, is a dwarf shrub used mainly for borders. *F. procumbens* has very decorative berries. There are a great many cultivars and hybrids with red, violet, orange and pinkish-white flowers, some being semidouble and some double.

37 FOTHERGILLA MAJOR
(syn. *F. alnifolia* var. *major, F. monticola*)   U.S. zone 6

Family Hamamelidaceae.

Place of origin Virginia to South Carolina.

Description This genus of deciduous shrubby plants was named after the distinguished British doctor John Fothergill (1712–80) and introduced into Europe toward the end of the 18th century.

F. major is a shrub, similar in appearance to a low-growing *Hamamelis* (Witch Hazel). It is sometimes dwarf but can range in height from 3–10 ft. (1–3 m.). Its stems and branches are covered with starry hairs. The simple, coarsely toothed, alternate leaves, borne on short stalks, turn yellow and then red in late autumn. Its showy, white flowers are carried in dense terminal spikes; their bracts appear in the spring at the same time as the leaves; the flowers have a 5- or 7-lobed campanulate calyx and showy stamens whose filaments are often prominent. This slow-growing shrub has a distinctive shape and is very decorative in the autumn garden.

Cultivation This is a hardy plant that grows well in a moist, cool position like that favored by azaleas. It likes a fairly peaty or sandy soil with plenty of organic material but lime-free. It can be planted in the autumn or early spring, before the buds appear, preferably in semishade where it will not become too dry during the summer. No pruning is needed but any excess branches should be removed after flowering in May to prevent the shrub from becoming overcrowded.

Winter protection No protection is necessary.

Propagation By layering of the flexible branches in October.

Other species *F. gardenii*, a fragrantly scented dwarf shrub.

38 GARDENIA JASMINOIDES

(syn. *G. florida, G. grandiflora*)
Gardenia, Cape Jasmine

Family Rubiaceae.

Place of origin China.

Description The gardenia acquired its name in honor of one of Linnaeus' botanical correspondents, the Scottish-American doctor and botanist Dr. Alexander Garden. The genus was introduced into Europe in 1761. It is a shrubby plant growing to 6 ft. (2 m.), with glossy, persistent leaves. It produces double, axillary, solitary, white flowers with waxy petals like those of a camellia and has a heady fragrance.

Cultivation Gardenias are lime-hating plants, like camellias, azaleas, etc., and prefer rainwater to tap water. In containers they need acid soil; if grown outdoors, a good proportion of well-broken-down leafmold and sand should be mixed into the soil first.

Winter protection In cold climates, gardenias must be brought under cover during the winter and should therefore be planted in large, well-drained pots. During the coldest months they should be kept in a dry, well-ventilated atmosphere with good light and no central heating. In the British Isles they need conservatory treatment.

Propagation By air layering which should be carried out immediately after flowering; the gardenia is reproduced commercially by cuttings but these take a long time to root.

Other species *G. thunbergia* a robust shrub from South Africa, with fragrant waxy-white flowers. Not hardy.

---

39 GENISTA CINEREA

Family Leguminosae.

Place of origin Southwest Europe.

Description An erect deciduous shrub up to 10 ft. (3 m.) in height, it has numerous long, pilose branches without spines and a grayish trunk. Its small gray-green leaves are lanceolate and alternate on the sterile branches and obovate on the fertile ones. Its numerous pilose, bright yellow flowers are united in loose axillary racemes along the branches. Its fruits consist of small silky, whitish pods. This shrub grows wild on the rocky, arid ground of the Mediterranean regions and is cultivated for the decorative quality of its brilliant yellow flowers and for the silky appearance of the whole plant.

Cultivation It likes to be warm and in full sun and thrives in poor, sandy, acid soil.

Propagation By seed in the spring, by cuttings in August.

Other species *G. hispanica* (Spanish Gorse), a low-growing, dense, spiny shrub with yellow flowers. *G. monosperma*, a shrub up to 13 ft. (4 m.) in height in the wild with white, scented flowers in racemes along the branches. In the British Isles it will only grow to 2–4 ft. (0.5–1 m.) *G. pilosa*, a lime-hating species with yellow flowers. *G. radiata*, with yellow flowers in terminal heads of 6 blossoms.

40   HIBISCUS SYRIACUS

Family   Malvaceae.
Place of origin   India and China.
Description   This well-known deciduous plant has been cultivated for over 400 years and used in many ways; for hedges, to
line paths, etc. Usually seen as a shrub, it is also sometimes
grown as a small tree. It reaches a height of 10–15 ft. (3–5 m.)
and has numerous alternate, cuneate-oval, gray leaves. Its
single or double flowers, which range in color from pink to
mauve and white are axillary and funnel-shaped with short
stems.
Cultivation   A hardy species, it prefers loamy, fairly damp soil
and a sunny position, although it also does well in semishade. In
cold areas it is advisable to plant it in the shelter of a wall.
Pruning should be carried out in February to remove dead wood
and stimulate the growth of new shoots. It is generally best to let
the plant grow freely since it tends to have a more interesting
appearance as it ages.
Propagation   By seed, by cuttings taken in the spring or
summer and rooted in sandy, peaty soil.
Other taxa   *H. syriacus* 'Alba Plena,' double white flowers; *H.
syriacus* 'Caeruleus Plenus,' double violet-colored flowers; *H.
syriacus* 'Violaceus Atropurpureus,' single purple flowers.

---

41   HIPPOPHAË RHAMNOIDES
Sea Buckthorn

Family   Elaeagnaceae.
Place of origin   Europe and temperate Asia.
Description   A well-branched dioecious, deciduous shrub that
reaches a height of about 30 ft. (10 m.), sometimes of arboreal
habit, with dense, spiny branchlets. Its narrow, alternate leaves
are linear and lanceolate, green on the upper surface and gray
on the lower. The small, greenish-yellow flowers are quite
insignificant; they appear with the leaves, the males with catkins
and the females axillary and solitary. The fruits are small, round,
orange-yellow berries; very rich in vitamin C; although their pulp
is acid, they are attractive to birds. The plant grows wild on sunny
hillsides, on the coast and by rivers. It is cultivated for the
decorative effect of its pale foliage and of its berries. It is used to
prevent soil erosion and for colonizing with its numerous
suckers.
Cultivation   Well-suited to poor, sandy, calcareous soil, this
plant is hardy and can withstand the frost. It thrives in a bright
sunny position and tolerates dryness when fully grown. It makes
an excellent hedge and is not damaged by being trimmed quite
hard several times in the summer. In planting, there should
always be one male to six females.
Propagation   By division of the root suckers, by cuttings.

42 HYDRANGEA MACROPHYLLA
Hydrangea

Family Hydrangeaceae.
Place of origin Japan.
Description A deciduous bushy shrub reaching a height of 12 ft. (4 m.), it is grown for the ornamental effect of its wide-spreading foliage and showy flowers, which turn blue in acid soil but remain pink in alkaline and calcareous soil. Its large, oval leaves have a toothed margin and are about 8 in. (20 cm.) long. The inflorescences are arranged in a large, round, terminal corymb consisting of colored sepals in flat groups of 4. The sterile flowers attract pollinating insects but there are no fertile flowers in the ornamental cultivars. The inflorescences remain showy throughout the winter even after they have dried on the plant.
Cultivation Hydrangeas prefer to be sited in semishade rather than in full sun and sheltered from the wind. They need a great deal of watering and thrive best in soil that is damp and rich in humus. The old stems should be cut right back to the base in spring. To encourage the flowers to turn pink in acid soil, lime can be applied around the roots; to turn them blue in chalky soil, a compound of aluminum can be used.
Winter protection Necessary in areas with long winters.
Propagation By cuttings.
Other taxa *H. macrophylla* 'Domotoi' and 'Rosea,' with pink flowers. *H. macrophylla* 'Blue Waves' and 'Coerulea,' with blue flowers. *H.* 'Ave Maria,' with white flowers. *H.* 'Hamburg,' *H.* 'Princess Beatrix,' *H.* 'Merveille,' with red flowers.

---

43 HYDRANGEA PANICULATA

Family Hydrangeaceae.
Place of origin China and Japan.
Description A deciduous shrub reaching a height of 6–10 ft. (2–3 m.) with abundant pilose branches. The oval, lanceolate leaves are often arranged in whorls of 3; they are light green, the lower surface being pilose and the margins dentate. The flowers are arranged in erect, conical, rather untidy terminal panicles about 12 in. (30 cm.) long. They consist of 4 white sepals that turn pink as they fade. The name of this genus derives from the Greek and refers to the cup-shaped fruits.
Cultivation This hydrangea requires deep, well-manured soil and tolerates lime; it prefers a warm site without direct sunlight and sheltered from the wind. The old branches should be cut back in spring to encourage the new flower buds.
Winter protection A very hardy plant that rarely needs protection.
Propagation By cuttings in the summer.
Other taxa *H. paniculata* 'Grandiflora' has larger flowers. *H. petiolaris* (Climbing Hydrangea), with white flowers, grows to about 50 ft. (16 m.) and tolerates cold winters.

44 ILEX AQUIFOLIUM
English Holly

Family Aquifoliaceae.
Place of origin Europe, North Africa, western Asia.
Description A bushy evergreen tree growing to 66 ft. (20 m.). The glossy dark green, leathery leaves are elliptic to oval and have sharp spines, tending to decrease on higher branches and on mature trees. The small, white, 4–5 petaled, unisexual flowers are grouped in axillary clusters and borne on separate male and female plants. The female plants produce bright red, round, poisonous berries.
Cultivation English holly grows well in all but the coldest parts of western Europe and in the Pacific Northwest of America, but is hard to grow successfully elsewhere in the U.S. It prefers a temperate climate, with well-drained, moisture-retentive, clayey, non calcareous soil and a sunny or semishaded, sheltered position. To ensure fruiting there should always be a few plants of each gender growing together. Holly responds well to trimming and can be used for hedging.
Propagation By cuttings in autumn, by layering or seed.
Other taxa There are many cultivars of *I. aquifolium* noted for their gold and silver variegation (often on leaf margin) and variety in shape, leaf size, habit and fruit color. *I. crenata*, an evergreen shrub with small leaves and blackfruits, often used for hedging. *I. cornuta* (Horned Holly), dense evergreen shrub, 5-spined leaves, large red berries. *I. opaca* (American Holly), evergreen tree to 50 ft. (15 m.), red fruits, native to eastern and central U.S. Likes a continental climate. *I. verticillata* (Black Alder), eastern U.S., deciduous shrub, showy in autumn, fruits red.

45 JASMINUM GRANDIFLORUM
Spanish Jasmine

Family Oleaceae.
Place of origin Unknown.
Description In all probability this was the jasmine that Vasco da Gama imported into Spain in 1548. It is a viny shrub growing to 15 ft. (5 m.) high and has light green, pinnate, opposite leaves or, more usually, groups of leaflets. Its large, single flowers are very sweetly scented; they are pink when in bud turning to white when open. The individual flowers are short-lived but the plant continues to flower from June to October and sometimes even during the winter.
Cultivation Spanish jasmine is grown commercially in many areas, since the well-known essence obtained from its flowers is used in the manufacture of some perfumes. It is a very delicate plant that dies if the temperature falls below 32°F (0°C). It requires a warm, sunny position and loose, sandy, organically rich soil. Spanish jasmine is often grown in pots so its owners can take it to their summer homes and continue to enjoy its wonderful fragrance.
Winter protection This species is suited only to warm climates; when grown in any other environment it must be protected or, if in a pot, put into the sunniest part of a greenhouse.
Propagation By cuttings, by simple layering, by air layering.
Other species *J. sambac* (Arabian Jasmine), which has a very delicate fragrance; *J. azoricum*, needs conservatory treatment; has sweetly scented white flowers.

46 JUNIPERUS COMMUNIS
Common Juniper

Family Cupressaceae.

Place of origin Europe, including Britain.

Description A woody, evergreen shrub branching up from the base. It is dense and bushy with an erect, pyramidal habit, attaining a height of up to 20 ft. (6 m.). At higher altitudes it adopts a prostrate habit. The juniper is very slow-growing. Its woody trunk is aromatic and reddish in color and the bark flakes off easily. Its needle-like, prickly leaves are ⅜–⅝ in. (10–15 mm.) long; they are persistent, growing in whorls of 3; their upper surface is whitish and the lower is gray-green. It is a dioecious plant. The male plant has a more cylindrical form and its flowers are small oval catkins. The little inflorescences of the female plant are green and insignificant. Its fruits are a glaucous green in the first year, becoming bluish black in the second as they ripen, ³⁄₁₆–⁵⁄₁₆ in. (5–8 mm.) in diameter, containing 3 seeds. The juniper grows wild in dry woodlands and wastelands to an altitude of about 8,200 ft. (2,500 m.).

It behaves like a pioneer plant in the uncultivated meadowlands and montane pastures, its spiny leaves giving it ample protection from herbivorous animals. Its roots are very efficient in preventing land slippage wherever the soil is loose, as on dry hillsides or windy beaches. It has been known and used as a medicinal plant since antiquity. Its fruits are also used in the making of liqueurs and gin.

Cultivation It grows in any kind of soil and tolerates dryness. It likes to be sited in a position with plenty of space and sun. The juniper is a very hardy plant that is not affected by frost, changes of temperature or hard pruning. It can be used in shrubberies or in a hedge, where it can be kept well-trimmed. It is very decorative in its shape and variety of leaves. It is easy to grow almost anywhere and is a great attraction to birds, which play an important part in the dissemination of its seeds.

Propagation Reproduction by seed is very slow but the plants produced in this way are the best. It can also be propagated by air layering and cuttings from young shoots.

Other taxa Differences in height and color of foliage: *J. chinensis* (Chinese juniper), a dioecious plant to 65 ft. (20 m.); probably poisonous; very decorative. *J.c. pfitzeriana*, (Pfitzer Juniper), is probably the most popular and useful juniper sold in the U.S.; a mainstay for foundation plantings, it grows to 10 ft. (3 m.) but is easily kept lower and is very hardy (zone 5). *J. oxycedrus* (Prickly Juniper), a shrub attaining 16–17 ft. (5 m.), distinguished by its large, reddish-blue fruit up to ⅜ in. (1 cm.) across; its wood is red. *J. oxycedrus* subsp. *macrocarpa* has slightly larger fruit ⅜–⅝ in. (10–15 mm.) across, less spiny leaves and curved branches. *J. phoenicia*, a poisonous shrub that is recognizable by its non prickly, squamiform leaves, this plant is typically Mediterranean with its dense foliage and large reddish-brown berries. *J. sabina* (Common Savin), a poisonous shrub, monoecious or dioecious, it is recognizable by its non prickly, squamiform leaves, its pendulous, violet-colored berries and its red bark that flakes off like scales. *J. virginiana* (Eastern Red Cedar), an ornamental North American tree reaching a height of 60 ft. (18 m.); its glaucous leaves are partly acicular and partly squamiform. In the U.S. it grows from the far north to the deep south.

47 KALMIA LATIFOLIA
Mountain Laurel, Calico Bush

U.S. zone 5

Family Ericaceae.
Place of origin Eastern U.S., New Brunswick to Florida.
Description *Kalmia* is the name of a genus that includes a small group of exclusively American species. Its flowers are so attractive that Connecticut and Pennsylvania have named the mountain laurel as their state flowers. *K. latifolia* is a dense, compact, more or less rounded, evergreen shrub with glossy green leaves that are poisonous to animals. The inflorescences consist of tiny white or very pale pink bells borne in terminal corymbs; they open in late spring and in good years they almost blanket the plants. In new cultivars that have been recently developed and are now widely available, the flowers are a much deeper pink and sometimes almost red. When not in bloom, the laurel is rather similar to a rhododendron.
Cultivation The mountain laurel, like the azalea, prefers a peaty, open soil that is fairly acid. It grows and blooms vigorously in sun or partial shade. It also grows in deep shade but does not bloom. Very little pruning is required.
   The shrub is easy to move but in the U.S. it is on the conservation list of most states in which it thrives, therefore nursery-grown specimens should be planted.
Winter protection None is required.
Propagation By simple layering of the flexible branches in summer.
Other species *K. angustifolia* (Sheep Laurel) is much smaller than mountain laurel and is recommended for use only in wet soil; the flowers are red.

---

48 KERRIA JAPONICA

U.S. zone 5

Family Rosaceae.
Place of origin China.
Description A deciduous shrub attaining a height of about 6½ ft. (2 m.) with long, slender branches that are green and pendulous. The ovate-lanceolate green leaves are about 4 in. (10 cm.) long, sharply pointed and alternate with a doubly toothed margin. The single yellow flowers supported by stalks, are large, solitary and terminal with a 5-petaled corolla. The fruits are dark nutlike clusters. *Kerria japonica* is grown as an ornamental plant for its early flowering and attractive foliage which turns yellow in the autumn. It was named after William Kerr, a young gardener from the Royal Botanic Gardens at Kew in England, who was sent to China in 1803.
Cultivation This shrub grows in any kind of soil and likes to be in full sun or semishade with some shelter in very cold areas. It is a hardy plant and is not affected by a polluted urban atmosphere. The branches that have borne flowers should be pruned out in the summer. A top dressing of manure should be given and the plants kept well watered in the spring.
Propagation By cuttings, by seed, by division of the root shoots, by simple layering or by air layering.
Other species *K. japonica* 'Variegata' ('Picta') with white-margined leaves; *K. japonica* 'Aureovariegata' with yellow-margined leaves; *K. japonica* 'Grandiflora' with large flowers; *K. japonica* 'Pleniflora' with large double yellow flowers; it needs to be planted in full sun.

49 KOLKWITZIA AMABILIS
Beauty Bush

U.S. zone 5

Family Caprifoliaceae.

Place of origin China.

Description A deciduous shrub with a bushy habit and dense foliage attaining a height of about 12 ft. (4 m.). The young branches, leaf stalks and fruits are all covered in thick down. Its broad, oval, dark green leaves are hairy with a slender point, toothed margin, and reticulate venation. Its flowers are pink on the outside and rather paler inside with yellow throats; gathered into clusters, they are bell-shaped, rather flattened at the base, and have 5 rounded petals. Its fruits are in capsule form containing seeds covered with a brown skin. The brown bark flakes off during the winter. The beauty bush, as its common name implies, is a very decorative, hardy plant, and the attractive flowers totally cover the arching branches. It makes fine patches of color in the June garden and is particularly suitable for hedging.

Cultivation Although slow-growing, this shrub does not present any difficulties. It likes a light, sunny position and grows in any type of soil provided that it is well-drained, rich and manured. It needs to be kept well-watered. It should be mulched before the summer weather starts to keep the roots cool and moist. When the flowering season ends, all the branches that have flowered can be pruned out and any others removed to avoid overcrowding. The plant can be pruned quite hard in the spring to remove any frost-damaged parts; it is, however, quite hardy and resistant to frost. A regular top dressing of manure before flowering is beneficial.

Winter protection Young plants need some protection in areas where the climate is severe.

Propagation By softwood cuttings in summer, by seed directly into the ground in spring.

Other species *K. amabilis* 'Rosea' and 'Pink Cloud' are cultivars that produce darker pink flowers.

50 LAVANDULA ANGUSTIFOLIA
(syn. *L. officinalis, L. vera, L. spica*)
Common Lavender

Family Labiatae.
Place of origin Western Mediterranean.
Description An evergreen subshrub that makes very decorative hedges and colorful clumps. It is cultivated for its medicinal properties and for its flowers, which not only attract bees and butterflies but are also used for their perfume. It grows wild, or has been allowed to revert to the wild, in hot Mediterranean regions. It is a bushy plant, densely branched from the base, with an overall rounded shape; it attains a height of about 3 ft. (1 m.). The linear, gray-green leaves are grouped in opposite pairs on woody stems. The tiny bluish-mauve, tubiform flowers are 2-lipped and densely grouped in whorls at the tip of erect, almost leafless stems to form terminal spikes. The flower stems grow taller than the leaf stems. The name of the genus derives from the ancient custom of using lavender to perfume soaps, from the Latin *lavare*, "to wash."
Cultivation Lavender is very easy to grow and flourishes in even the poorest soil as long as it is well-drained. It likes a hot, sunny position but is fairly resistant to the cold. It can be cut back quite hard after flowering.
Propagation By cuttings of the most recent wood taken in the spring or autumn and rooted in a damp, shady position; by seed.
Other species *L. dentata*, in which the floral spike is smaller, although flowering continues throughout the summer. *L. stoechas* (French Lavender), a Mediterranean low-growing, strongly scented shrub.

---

51 LEYCESTERIA FORMOSA

Family Caprifoliaceae.
Place of origin The Himalayas, western China, eastern Tibet.
Description This genus was introduced into Europe at the beginning of the 19th century when the first plants were introduced from the Himalayas. There it grows at altitudes ranging between 1,600–11,500 ft. (500–3,500 m.). A deciduous shrub, 3–6 ft. (1–2 m.) high, with rather large ovate leaves. Its small tubiform white flowers, with reddish-purple bracts, appear in the mid summer. When the leaves have fallen in winter, the stems are seen to resemble bamboo canes.
Cultivation *Leycesteria* is hardy and very easy to grow. It thrives in any soil, even calcareous, regardless of whether it is in full sun or semishade. If the weather is dry, the plant should be watered often and be well-mulched with damp peat. To achieve green stems during the winter the shoots should be cut back in March to two or three buds from their base.
Propagation By softwood cuttings rooted in the spring; by seed sown in the spring.
Other species *L. crocothyrsos*, a less hardy species with yellow flowers; it originates from Assam and except for the mildest districts should be kept in a cool greenhouse.

52 LIGUSTRUM OVALIFOLIUM
Oval Leaf Privet

Family Oleaceae.

Place of origin Japan.

Description Privet is a plant much written about by Latin writers and its flower is recorded in some of the epigrams of the poet, Martial, who lived in Rome in the first century AD. In its wild state it grows in scrublands and hedgerows. It has naturalized itself in parts of Europe, Asia and North America. A shrub about 15 ft. (5 m.) high with flexible branches, from which characteristic the name of the genus seems to derive – the Latin *ligare*, meaning "to bind or tie up." It has a more or less rounded form. Its semipersistent, ovate leaves have short stalks. The small, white, 4-petaled flowers are gathered into terminal panicles and are heavily scented; they are very attractive to bees. Its fruits are round, black berries and are relished by thrushes, blackbirds and other berry-eating birds. Privet is useful in preventing soil erosion and as a pioneer plant in reforestation.

Cultivation This shrub likes a calcareous soil and constant moisture; it thrives in a sunny or shady position and withstands the cold well. It can also be grown in a pot. It makes an excellent hedge and tolerates severe trimming; when creating a hedge space the plants at intervals of 20 in. (50 cm.).

Propagation Growing from seed is a slow process. Quicker methods are: by simple layering, by division of root suckers, by cuttings taken in the autumn.

Other species *L. japonicum* 'Rotundifolium,' with round ever-green leaves and scented flowers in terminal panicles. *L. lucidum*, a small tree attaining a height of about 16 ft. (5 m.), with persistent, glossy, leathery leaves. *L. vulgare* (Common Privet), a deciduous shrub with abundant flowers.

53 MAHONIA AQUIFOLIUM
Oregon Grape

Family Berberidaceae.

Place of origin North America.

Description An evergreen shrub grown for its beautiful glossy foliage, showy racemes of flowers and attractive, grapelike clusters of dark berries. It is a woody plant, rarely more than 3 ft. (1 m.) in height, with prostrate or ascendant branches. The pinnate leaves consist of 5–9 ovate leaflets about 2 in. (5 cm.) long on red stalks; they are dark green and shiny with a serrate margin that undulates and has spiny teeth, similar to, but softer than the leaves of the English holly, from which it derives its specific name. The genus is named for the 19th-century North American horticulturist Bernard McMahon.

Its sweetly scented, yellow flowers are gathered into rather loose, erect racemes; the corolla is cup-shaped, like that of the barberry, consisting of 6 petals and containing stamens which, when touched, release their pollen on to the stigma. The round, blackish fruits, which are edible and can be used in the same way as the fruit of the barberry, have a bloom on their skins like black grapes; the pulp is red. This shrub is occasionally found growing wild as a result of either natural dissemination or of spreading of its numerous suckers.

Cultivation *Mahonia* grows well in semishade or even in full shade. It is ideal for filling in the lower part of a shrubbery or in shady garden spots. It prefers damp, calcareous, mineral-rich soil and benefits from a good dressing of manure in the spring. It does not like frost and grows well in a mild climate. Pruning should be carried out after flowering since *Mahonia* blooms on the previous year's wood; the branches that have flowered can be cut back to the second bud to prevent the plant from getting too big. If there is plenty of space around the *Mahonia* it can be allowed to grow without being cut back thus allowing the fruits to develop. This plant can be grown in a pot to decorate a sheltered terrace or balcony during the winter.

Winter protection The *Mahonia* should be given some protection during long cold spells.

Propagation By seed in autumn, by division of the root suckers in autumn or spring, by softwood cuttings in autumn.

Other species *M. bealei.* originating from China, has bluish-black berries. *M. japonica*, originating from Japan, is about 6½ ft. (2 m.) high with erect branches and leathery leaves consisting of 13–19 leaflets. *M. lomariifolia*, originating from China and Burma, is about 10 ft. (3 m.) high with long leaves consisting of 9½–18½ leaflets; it flowers in the winter and can be tender, suitable for warm climates. *M. repens* (Creeping Mahonia), originating from North America, is a low-growing, creeping shrub, used as ground cover. There is also a hybrid of *M. aquifolium* and *Berberis vulgaris* (Barberry) known as *M.* × *Mahoberberis neubertii*, which has large, toothed leaves and does not bear flowers.

54 MIMOSA PUDICA
Sensitive Plant

Family Leguminosae.
Place of origin Brazil.
Description The name "mimosa," from the Latin *mimos*, meaning a "mimic actor," would appear to have been given to this genus because of its mimic or camouflage qualities. If something brushes even lightly against the leaves, they fold up on themselves, while the stalk reacts by folding downward, taking with it the folded leaf. This collapse is only temporary and after about a half-hour the plant returns to its normal state.

It is a semiclimbing, prickly evergreen shrub reaching a height of 16½ ft. (5 m.). The light green leaves, borne on 4-in. (10-cm.) stems, are bipinnate and divided into several sections, each one of which is further subdivided into many little leaflets. From early summer to late autumn pale pink flowers in clusters of 5–8 spring from the leaf axils on short stalks.
Cultivation *M. pudica* is a perennial plant if grown under the right conditions. It requires a warm climate and will not withstand winter frosts. It likes a position that is sheltered from the wind and needs to be well-watered.
Winter protection If the plant is not in a really temperate-hot atmosphere, or is not growing in a pot that can be taken indoors, it should be well-protected from the cold weather.
Propagation By seed in early spring.

---

55 MYRTUS COMMUNIS
Common Myrtle

Family Myrtaceae.
Place of origin Western Asia.
Description An evergreen shrub or, occasionally, small tree attaining a height of 10 ft. (3 m.). It grows wild in the coastal and submontane Mediterranean regions but it is believed to have been introduced there. Its woody stems are erect and its young branchlets tetragonal. The glossy, waxy, persistent leaves are sessile, opposite or, rarely, in whorls of 3; they are oval with a pointed tip, dark green on the upper surface and lighter on the lower, with prominent central venation and an entire margin. The leaves are punctuated by glands that emit a characteristic fragrance when brushed against. The white flowers also have a distinctive aroma; they grow singly or in groups, on long stalks from the leaf axils; there are two opposite caducous bracts over the calyx and the corolla consists of 5 rounded, well-separated petals with numerous white stamens and yellow anthers. The fruit is a blue-black, ovoidal, aromatic berry crowned by the remains of the calyx.
Cultivation Myrtle is a heat-loving plant and grows well in a warm climate in any soil. It likes a warm position in full sun. It grows slowly and is long-lived.
Winter protection In cold areas myrtle is best grown, or at least overwintered, in a frost-free greenhouse or conservatory.
Propagation By seed, by division of the suckers.
Other species There are numerous cultivars and species, both wild and cultivated, which can be distinguished by the size of their leaves.

56 NERIUM OLEANDER

(syn. *N. oderum*)
Oleander

Family Apocynaceae.

Place of origin Mediterranean regions.

Description An evergreen shrub attaining a height of about 16 ft. (5 m.). The bark, leaves and seeds are poisonous. With its thick, colorful growth it is quite spectacular in its natural habitat along gravelly seashores and on the sunny sloping banks of mountain streams. The liking of the oleander for water is reflected in the name of the genus which derives from the Greek *neros*. Its long, lanceolate leaves are leathery with parallel venation and arranged in whorls of 2–3.

The pink or white flowers are grouped in terminal clusters and are delightfully scented; they are funnel-shaped with 5 broad lobes with laciniate fauces. Its long fruit opens into 2 valves containing pilose seeds.

Cultivation The oleander likes a warm, sunny position and good loamy soil. It can be grown in a deep pot. It needs to be well watered during the vegetative period.

Winter protection This is necessary in a cold climate. Oleander is not hardy in the British Isles.

Propagation By seed, by cuttings, by air layering, by simple layering, and by grafting.

---

57 OLEARIA ERUBESCENS

Family Compositae.

Place of origin Tasmania, Australia.

Description This is an evergreen shrub that ranges in height from 28 in. to 5 ft. (0.7–1.5 m.). It has long, slender branches covered with silky red-brown down like the lower surface of the leaves. These are dark green, alternate, rigid and leathery, oval and oblong, rounded at the base and sharply toothed with a short stalk. The flowers, which appear in May and June, are in solitary capitula or in groups. They consist of 3 or 5 white radial flowers with 6–8 yellow ones in the center.

Cultivation This species is suited only to temperate climates. It prefers a light, acid soil enriched with organic material of a peaty or leafmold type. In very warm weather it likes to be in semi-shade but prefers sun otherwise.

Winter protection This is necessary if temperatures fall much below 20°F (−6°C).

Propagation By seed, by cuttings.

Other species *O.* × *haastii* is the most commonly grown species in the U.S. Growing to 9 ft. (3 m.) tall, it may spread to as much as 15 ft. (5 m.). *O. semidentata*, a splendid shrub with silvery leaves and lilac flowers.

58 OLEARIA PHLOGOPAPPA
(syn. *O. gunniana*)

U.S. zone 8

Family Compositae.
Place of origin Tasmania, Australia.
Description A fine flowering shrub although not very resistant to frost, reaching a height of 6–10 ft. (2–3 m.). It is very ramified and has opaque, obovate leaves with white beneath. Its capitula are produced in profusion in racemose corymbs at the top of the branched stems. The flowers are pure white with a yellow, daisy-like center. There are also cultivars with mauve or deep pink flowers known as the 'Splendens' group.
Cultivation An evergreen shrub, suitable for temperate climates. It is a lime-hater and prefers light, acid, sandy soil enriched with peat or leafmold. In a very hot climate a partially shaded position is preferable.
Winter protection Where there is the possibility of frost, these plants should be overwintered in a cold greenhouse.
Propagation By seed in the spring, in a temperate greenhouse. By cuttings taken in the summer and rooted in a sandy soil, overwintering in a coldframe or greenhouse. Rooting of the young wood can be encouraged by using a heated propagating frame.

59 OPUNTIA FICUS-INDICA
Indian Fig Cactus

U.S. zone 9

Family Cactaceae.
Place of origin Origin unknown.
Description A spiny shrub up to about 16 ft. (5 m.) tall with a rounded trunk. Its fleshy, succulent, green branches known as "blades," are ascendant and erect, with an oval shape and without leaves. The surfaces of the blades are punctuated by small protuberances containing clumps of long, yellow spines. The flowers, situated on the margins of the blades, are about 4 in. (10 cm.) across and have numerous yellow petals and stamens. The fruits are large, oval, yellow or red berries, flat at the apex and spiny, about 4 in. (10 cm.) long; they are edible and sweet to the taste. There are numerous seeds in the fruit. This cactus is widely naturalized in tropical and subtropical areas. It is often grown as a protective hedge, to mark boundaries.
Cultivation The Indian fig cactus is able to grow in dry, poor soil provided that it is in a warm-to-hot position in full sun. It is not suitable as a pot plant. It thrives only in regions where the climate is hot and it tolerates dryness very well.
Propagation By seed or by detaching a blade and planting it.
Other species *Nopalea cochenillifera* (*O. cochenillifera*, Cochineal Cactus), originating from Central America, on which the cochineal insect feeds, from which creature the red cochineal dye is obtained. It has tapering blades and large red flowers. *O. vulgaris* (Prickly Pear), originating from South America, has insipid fruits and large yellow flowers. *O. microdasys* and *O. basilaris* are dwarf species, very suitable for rocky gardens where the soil is poor.

60 OSMANTHUS FRAGRANS

Family Oleaceae.
Place of origin China, Japan.
Description An elegant, dense evergreen shrub rather like an olive tree, with glossy foliage. Sometimes of arborescent habit, it is grown in regions with a mild climate. The opposite, leathery leaves are about 2¼–4 in. (6–10 cm.) long, lanceolate or elliptic with a serrate margin. The white flowers are borne on short stems and grouped into clusters at the leaf axils. The main bloom period is in the spring and the second in the autumn. The flowers have a strong fragrance reminiscent of peaches. Its fruits are oval, purplish-blue drupes, rather like olives.
Cultivation *Osmanthus* is easy to grow. It needs a sunny position on well-drained, acid, organic soil and is well-suited to a mild climate. To retain its buoyant and elegant appearance it should be pruned only to remove tangled or overcrowded branches. It cannot be grown outdoors in the British Isles.
Propagation By seed in the spring, by air layering, by softwood cuttings in July.
Other species *O. fragrans* forma *aurantiacus* is the orange-flowered form of the above species. *O. delavayi*, originating from China, is hardy and evergreen with little white, fragrant flowers in the spring. *O. heterophyllus* (*O. aquifolium, O. ilicifolius*) is a hardy evergreen shrub from Japan with holly-like leaves especially when juvenile. Fragrant, white flowers are produced in September–October followed by oblong blue fruits. There are several cultivars. Often used for hedging.

---

61 PACHYSANDRA TERMINALIS
Pachysandra

Family Buxaceae.
Place of origin Japan.
Description A semiwoody evergreen subshrub with a creeping habit, its stems elongating into subterranean rhizomes. It is only about 12 in. (30 cm.) high. Its green, stemmed leaves can be up to about 3 in. (8 cm.) long; they are obovate, toothed toward the tip. The white petalless flowers, although quite insignificant individually, are made more decorative by the way in which they are gathered into terminal spikes 1–2 in. (3–5 cm.) long.
Cultivation This plant grows in any kind of soil provided it is rich in minerals and organic materials. It likes a shady position and is resistant to the cold. *Pachysandra* is usually grown as a groundcover because it crowds out most weeds, spreads rapidly and develops into a luxuriant carpet. It can be planted at almost any time during warm weather and should be given a top dressing of fertilizer regularly in the spring and autumn.
Propagation By root division in the spring.
Other species *P. terminalis* 'Variegata' whose leaves have a white margin. *P. procumbens* originating from North America, is a deciduous plant whose ill-scented flowers appear before its leaves.

62 PAEONIA SUFFRUTICOSA
Tree Peony, Moutan   U.S. zone 6

Family Ranunculaceae.

Place of origin China.

Description The peony is one of the most fascinating shrubs for any garden. The elegant flowers of the cultivated taxa are equaled by few other shrubs. At one time the plant was to be seen in many gardens but it is less popular today, perhaps because of the brevity of its spring flowering period. To the Chinese the cultivation of peonies developed into an art form and they succeeded in producing over 300 cultivars with white, pink and purple flowers. In fact, the tree peony became known in Europe through Chinese art and the descriptions brought back by missionaries long before the plant itself was introduced.

It is a deciduous shrub with an erect habit, attaining a height of 6–7 ft. (2 m.). The trunk is knotty and branched. The peony is slow-growing and does not flower until several years after planting. The leaves are about 12 in. (30 cm.) in length on long stalks and consist of 3 or 5 hairless leaflets. The scented flowers are single and between 4–8 in. (10–20 cm.) across in a range of colours including deep pink, pale pink, violet and yellow.

Cultivation Peonies are easy to grow in any soil although they do not like it to be too light or alkaline. They prefer a partially shaded position that is protected from the wind; full sun is to be avoided and it is therefore advisable to site the young plants in the shade of other shrubs. They can withstand the frost except in the spring when the new shoots are beginning to emerge. An autumn dressing of manure is beneficial. The plants should be mulched in May with well-rotted humus to keep them moist.

Propagation By division of the crowns in the autumn. By taking cuttings of the mature wood, with a heel, about 6–8 in. (15–20 cm.) long in September–October and dipping them in a rooting powder before setting them to root.

Other species *P. delavayi*, originating from China, a quick-growing shrub with pendulous blood-red flowers. *P. lutea*, with yellow flowers.

63　PELARGONIUM ZONALE
Zonal Pelargonium　　　　　　　　　　　　　　U.S. zone 9

Family　Geraniaceae.
Place of origin　South Africa.
Description　These are often incorrectly called "geraniums" although they in fact belong to a completely different genera; the flowers of the true *Geranium* are nearly always regular while those of the *Pelargonium* are generally irregular, the two upper petals of the latter differing from the others in size, shape, and sometimes color too. In addition *Pelargonium* is found almost exclusively in South Africa while *Geranium* is found over a much wider area.

The zonal pelargonium is a bushy plant with light green, succulent young growth. The round or cordate leaves are borne on long stalks and have a dark horseshoe-shaped medial zone. The inflorescences consist of globose umbels 6½ in. (16 cm.) in diameter composed of several individual flowers each borne on a rigid stem.
Cultivation　This pelargonium can withstand dryness although it is greatly improved by high atmospheric humidity. It requires a warm climate to survive throughout the year in open ground outdoors. It is not hardy in the British Isles and will require conservatory treatment. If bedded outside in the summer months it must be taken indoors at the first sign of frost. It grows best where the soil pH is between 6 and 7, well-mixed with leafmold and an annual dressing of manure.
Propagation　Usually by cuttings.
Other species　*P. odoratissimum*, *P. tomentosum*, *P. graveolens*, all with scented foliage.

64　PHILADELPHUS CORONARIUS
Mock Orange　　　　　　　　　　　　　　　　U.S. zone 6

Family　Philadelphaceae.
Place of origin　Southern Europe, Asia Minor.
Description　A deciduous shrub attaining a height of about 10 ft. (3 m.), it is very decorative with sweetly scented white flowers. The opposite, ovate leaves are up to 3¼ in. (8 cm.) long, slightly hairy beneath, with a sharply pointed tip and distinctive venation. Its creamy-white, strongly scented flowers are arranged in loose racemes; their 4-petaled corolla is supported by the 4 lobes of the calyx and they have numerous stamens and 4 styles. The fruit consists of a capsule divided into 4 parts.
Cultivation　The mock orange requires well-drained, well-manured soil. It is very hardy and very resistant to frost. It needs to be kept well-watered in dry weather. It can be pruned really hard in the spring to encourage regrowth or, alternatively, branches that have flowered can be cut back to the new shoots in July to prevent the shrub from becoming too dense. To make a hedge, the young plants should be spaced at intervals of 24 in. (60 cm.).
Propagation　By softwood cuttings in the summer or by hardwood cuttings in the autumn; by seed.
Other taxa　*P. coronarius* 'Aureus' with golden-yellow leaves. *P.* 'Manteau d'Hermine' with scented double flowers; this is a dwarf shrub suitable for hedging. *P.* 'Avalanche' with single white flowers. *P.* × 'Belle Étoile', white flowers flushed with red in the center. *P.* × *virginalis* with double white, scented flowers. *P. inodorus* with white, unscented flowers.

65 PHYLLOSTACHYS AUREA
Golden Bamboo

U.S. zone 7

Family Gramineae.
Place of origin China.
Description An evergreen shrub, often attaining a height of about 100 ft. (30 m.) in its natural habitat in the equatorial zone, but only about 12–25 ft. (4–8 m.) in temperate climates. It grows in bushy clumps or in isolation. The shoots, which spring from creeping rhizomes, are tender and edible when young. However, these soon become sheathed in a hollow yellow membrane that divides into tubular sections united by nodes. The basal nodes are very crowded, while 2 lateral branches emerge from each of the upper ones. The wall of the tubiform stem is smooth, woody, silicic and very strong. Its flexible branches bear large, narrow, linear leaves with reticulate venation. The flowers are gathered into abundant loose panicles of 2 or more; flowering is rare but occurs regularly and simultaneously throughout the world to the whole genus; sometimes plants die as a result. The fruit consists of a caryopsis. Bamboo cane is very tough and is often used in place of wood.
Cultivation This is a hardy plant that likes a cool, shady position in moist ground. It can also be grown in pots.
Propagation By springtime division of the clumps that originate from the underground rhizomes.
Other species *P. flexuosa*, from China, has an undulate stem. *P. hetrocycla* (*P. mitis*) from China, has caducous bracts along the cylindrical culms and slender, graceful branches. *P. nigra* (Black Bamboo); its stems are first olive green with a white waxy bloom, later turning a glossy dark, blackish color.

66 PHYTOLACCA AMERICANA
(syn. *P. decandra*)
Poke Weed

U.S. zone 6

Family Phytolaccaceae.
Place of origin North America.
Description A vigorous perennial growing 3–10 ft. (1–3 m.) high, with a ridged, dichotomous, erect stem that branches out at the top. Both stem and branches are a distinctive reddish color. It has large, whitish, rather fleshy taproots that are poisonous. The oval-acute, petiolate leaves with reddish venation turn purple in the autumn as do the flowers and buds, giving the whole plant a particularly attractive appearance in autumn. When the flowers first appear they are whitish, gradually suffusing to a delicate pink and then darkening; they are numerous and arranged in long, cylindrical, extra-axillary and subterminal clusters. The berrylike fruits, each consisting of 10 carpels, are glossy purplish-violet with crimson pulp.
Cultivation Grow in fertile, moisture retentive soil in sun or semishade. It is quick-growing under the right conditions.
Winter protection Fairly sensitive to the cold, however, it can sometimes be overwintered by ensuring that it is in light, loamy soil, well-protected from the north and east winds, and by giving its base a good covering of straw.
Propagation By seed.
Other species *P. dioica*, a tree about 20–23 ft. (6–7 m.) high with luxuriant foliage and hermaphrodite flowers borne on long petioles in pendulous racemes; of South American origin, it grows fast and is planted for decoration and shade.

67 PIERIS FORMOSA
(syn. *Andromeda formosa*)   U.S. zone 7

Family   Ericaceae.
Place of origin   The southern regions of the Himalayas through to parts of China.
Description   A well-proportioned, very compact evergreen shrub that can attain a height of 20 ft. (6 m.). Its leathery, oblong-lanceolate leaves are acuminate at both ends and finely toothed; the upper surface is a glossy deep green but paler beneath. Its pure white, urn-shaped flowers are pendulous and gathered into terminal panicles.
Cultivation   A shrub that looks particularly well in garden beds, it is grown in a neutral or slightly acid soil, in semishade or sun. If the branches become too dense, they can be thinned out after flowering and any branches that have grown too long can be cut back at the same time. Dead wood should also be removed, but little pruning is required.
Propagation   By simple layering in the autumn; by cuttings in late summer, rooted in a sand or peat mixture or in autumn when they should be put in a propagating frame. Also by seed.
Other taxa   *P. japonica* is of a less rigid and erect habit with almost pendulous branches and flowers in March–April. Often subject to frost so needs a sheltered spot. *P. formosa* var. *forestii* from China and Burma has several good clones with brilliant young foliage: 'Wakehurst' a shrub to 18 ft. (6 m.) and 'Forest Flame.' *P. floribunda* grows to 6 ft. (2 m.) and has white flowers that are produced in March–April. Very hardy.

---

68 PISTACIA LENTISCUS
Mastic   U.S. zone 8

Family   Anacardiaceae.
Place of origin   Mediterranean regions, Atlantic, Morocco and the Canary Islands.
Description   An evergreen shrub, sometimes bushy and sometimes a small tree, attaining a height of 20 ft. (6 m.). An aromatic, astringent lymph exudes from incisions in the stem; this is known as "lentisc mastic" and is used in flavoring, varnish, perfume and chewing gum. Its dark green, leathery, alternate leaves are paripinnate with 4–10 narrow lanceolate leaflets; they are glossy on the upper surface. Its inflorescences, consisting of red dioecious flowers, are grouped in axillary spikes. Its fruits are globose, aromatic and pea-size, ripening from red to black.
Cultivation   It thrives in a dry, warm climate in a sunny position and in any type of deep, well-aerated soil. It is suitable for creating thick, bushy clumps to give shade or for hedging in coastal gardens. It cannot withstand the cold.
Propagation   By seed in the spring or by division of the suckers.
Other species   *P. terebinthus*, a deciduous shrub from whose resin turpentine is obtained; its leaves are imparipinnate and its fruits hang in dense, showy racemes of red then purplish-brown drupes. *P. vera*, a small deciduous tree with hard fruits containing the edible, greenish seeds known as pistachio nuts. *P. terebinthus* can be grown in open ground in the British Isles, but the other species will need the protection of a wall.

69 PITTOSPORUM TOBIRA
Tobira

U.S. zone 8

Family Pittosporaceae.
Place of origin China, Japan and Korea.
Description A distinctive shrub, very attractive for its glossy, evergreen foliage, its compact shape, its long flowering period and the delicate fragrance of its flowers, which is especially delightful at dusk. Numerous branches spring from its woody stem giving a bushy appearance to the plant, which sometimes has the habit of a small tree and can reach a height of about 20 ft. (6 m.). Its obovate or lanceolate leaves are glossy, dark green on the upper surface and lighter beneath. Its creamy-white, sweetly scented flowers are arranged in numerous dense terminal inflorescences. Each floret has a 5-toothed calyx and 5 waxy petals. The resinous seeds account for the name of the genus which, in Greek, means "seed of pitch."
Cultivation This plant grows in regions where the winters are mild, especially near the coast or lakes, and it likes to be sited in full sun. It should be planted in the autumn. In warm climates it can be used to create a hedge. Pruning should be done in the autumn.
Propagation By seed, by cuttings.
Other species *P. eriocarpum*, from the Himalayas, with scented flowers and whitish, velutinate branches. *P. phylliraeoides*, originating from Australia, with solitary flowers, narrow leaves and pendulous branches. *P. revolutum*, with long leathery leaves and yellow flowers. *P. undulatum*, with fragrant leaves and white flowers. *P. viridiflorum*, from South Africa, with yellow flowers scented similarly to jasmine.

---

70 PLUMBAGO AURICULATA
(syn. ***Plumbago capensis***)
Cape Leadwort, Cape Plumbago

U.S. zone 8

Family Plumbaginaceae.
Place of origin South Africa.
Description A semiclimbing bushy plant with woody stems, growing to about 8 ft. (3.6 m.). Its light green, oblong leaves are smooth and entire. Its prolific sky-blue flowers are borne terminally on the branches in umbelliferous inflorescences; the calyx is hairy and the tubiform corolla at least three times its length.
Cultivation A rather delicate plant that cannot withstand frost. It grows well in any well-drained soil. It responds well to regular applications of liquid fertilizer throughout the summer.
Winter protection In regions where the winters are cold, leadwort is usually grown in large pots so that it can be brought into a well-ventilated, cool atmosphere of not more than 37–46°F (3–8°C) during the coldest months. Even in a mild climate, where it is grown outdoors, it is sometimes necessary to put some straw or peat around the roots. In these circumstances it is advisable to prune hard in the autumn and lightly in the spring, as soon as the plant shows signs of life, in order to hold it back until the worst of the cold weather and winds have passed.
Propagation By cuttings taken in the autumn from plants grown outdoors and in the spring from greenhouse plants. Also by crown division.
Other species *P. indica* (*P. rosea*), from Asia, has red flowers, ideal as a pot plant.

71 POLEMONIUM CAERULEUM
Jacob's Ladder

U.S. zone 7

Family Polemoniaceae.
Place of origin Northern hemisphere.
Description A bushy perennial about 34 in. (85 cm.) high with simple, hollow stems covered with tiny hairs, often tinged with red. Its leaves consist of 7–13 lanceolate leaflets on a slightly alate stalk. Its numerous flowers, often grouped together at the top of the stems, are borne on slightly downward-curving tomentose stems and the calyces are goblet-shaped with a rotate corolla. As soon as each flower starts to open, the anthers are already mature, and curve down toward the lower, marginal part of the corolla; as the stigma is beneath the anthers this facilitates self-pollination. The ripe fruits are carried erect and the trigonal, slightly winged seeds are dispersed on the wind. There are several cultivars that differ both in leaf shape and flower color, which ranges from sky-blue to salmon-pink.
Cultivation It thrives in any good soil (but prefers a well-drained loam) in a climate that is neither too wet nor too dry. *P. caeruleum* is usually grown in large clumps in grassy areas and flower beds. If cut back to ground level immediately after flowering, it will nearly always flower again in the autumn.
Propagation By seed or by crown division in the spring or autumn.
Other species *P. pauciflorum*, yellow flowers, from Mexico.

72 PRUNUS LAUROCERASUS
Cherry Laurel

U.S. zone 6

Family Rosaceae.
Place of origin Western Asia.
Description A vigorous evergreen shrub attaining a height of about 20 ft. (6 m.). It is grown mainly for its lustrous foliage but it also makes an excellent hedge. Its leathery, smooth, glossy leaves are about 4 in. (10 cm.) long and glandulous at the base of the lamina; they are obovate and lanceolate in shape. The scented white flowers, which are poisonous, are grouped close together in pyramidal, erect racemes, each flower having 5 petals. The fruits are black, oval drupes.
Cultivation Cherry laurel (especially the low-growing cultivars) is hardy and can withstand the cold. It grows quickly and does not object to lack of sun; it likes deep, moist topsoil but does not thrive in dry conditions. It is useful for hedging and as a windbreak.
Propagation By seed, by softwood cuttings in the summer.
Other taxa *P. laurocerasus* 'Caucasica,' large, dark green leaves. *P. laurocerasus* 'Magnoliifolia,' with extra large leaves. *P. laurocerasus* 'Otinii,' with very dark leaves, tree-flowering. *P. lusitanica* (Portuguese Laurel), a shrub particularly suitable for hedging and as a windbreak, with pendulous, scented flowers and conical purple fruits.

73 PONCIRUS TRIFOLIATA

U.S. zone 6

Family Rutaceae.

Place of origin China and Korea.

Description A deciduous tree or shrub to 35 ft. (11 m.) covered with straight, sharp spines and a crowded head of angular branches. Its leaves are trifoliate, with a terminal leaflet the same size as the two on each side of it; they are oblong-obtuse and borne on slightly alate petioles. Its large, white flowers are unscented; the corollas open before the leaves appear, their flat petals narrowing down to a basal claw; the stamens are free and the ovary is velvety. The fruits have a strong fragrance and a dark lemon-yellow skin; they are shaped rather like small oranges but are covered with very fine hairs. There is also an abundance of oleiferous glands in the skins. There is almost no pulp because the numerous ovoid seeds, which have a white embryo, allow little space for it, and the fruit is inedible because it is so bitter and intensely acid.

P. trifoliata is greatly appreciated by the Japanese in their cultivation of "bonsai." It makes a good hedging shrub and is ideal for marking the boundaries of a property as it forms an impenetrable barrier of thorns. It is also used ornamentally but its main use is as a stock on to which lemons, mandarins and oranges are grafted. In addition, it has produced a number of hybrids.

Cultivation It loves the sun and to be sited in a warm position but it also gives good results in semishade. It can withstand temperatures down to about 9–0°F (−15–−20°C). It thrives in any deep, loamy, well-drained soil. It can be left to develop naturally but does not object to being pruned, even quite hard, although the more severely it is cut back the fewer the flowers and fruits. In a hedge the young plants should be spaced at intervals of 20–24 in. (50–60 cm.). It is not used for hedging in the British Isles.

Propagation By seed sown in a seedbed in March. By softwood cuttings rooted in a coldframe between June and July; when well-rooted the young plants can be planted out the following spring.

Other species P. trifoliata is the only species in the genus.

74 PYRACANTHA COCCINEA
Scarlet Firethorn

Family Rosaceae.
Place of origin Southern Europe, Near East.
Description A very decorative evergreen shrub, ideal for hedging and for covering walls, pergolas etc. During the winter its persistent fruits make it particularly ornamental. The name of the genus derives from the Greek words, *pyr*, meaning "fire" and *akantha*, "thorn," referring to its bright red berries and to its spiny branches, which grow from central stems to a length of about 6 ft. (2 m.). Its alternate, leathery, shiny leaves are lanceolate-elliptic in shape, about 1½ in. (4 cm.) long with an entire margin. The little flowers have 5 petals and are grouped in inflorescences of dense, untidy panicles. The fruits are small, round, red berries that remain on the plant virtually throughout the winter if they are not all eaten by birds.
Cultivation The firethorn grows in dry soil of any type. It is hardy and resistant to the cold but does not like prolonged dryness. It thrives in a sheltered position in full sun or semishade. It is one of the genera in the Rosaceae that is extremely prone to fireblight. Pruning should be carried out regularly and it requires support if it is to be trained up a high wall or pergola. To make a hedge, space the young plants at intervals of 24 in. (60 cm.).
Propagation By seed in open ground, by cuttings in the summer.
Other taxa *P. coccinea* 'Lalandei,' suitable for compact hedges. *P. angustifolia*, evergreen with creamy-white flowers and orange-yellow fruit. *P. crenulata*, a rather smaller plant with less resistance to the cold. *P. rogersiana*, originating from China, is a spiny shrub with smaller leaves and golden-yellow berries.

75 RHAMNUS ALATERNUS
(syn. **R.** *alaternus* var. *latifolius*)
Mediterranean Buckthorn

Family Rhamnaceae.
Place of origin Mediterranean region, Portugal, Atlantic, Morocco and the Crimea.
Description A spineless evergreen shrub with a dense, compact head that attains a height of about 16 ft. (5 m.). Its branches are erect and alternate, giving off a distinctive, rather unpleasant odor when freshly cut. Its leathery alternate leaves are dark green on the upper surface, ovate, lanceolate and rotund in shape with an entire or dentate margin. The flowers, in rounded, axillary racemes, are either male or female and have an unpleasant odor; the florets are yellow, the female being erect and the male pendulous. The fruits, which attract birds, are small round drupes that turn from red to black as they ripen; they contain 3 inedible nuts.
Cultivation This is a hardy plant that adapts to any light, poor, even clayey or sandy soil. It likes a sunny position. A very long-lived plant, it is often grown as a hedge in seaside gardens. It does not like cold winds but does well near the sea.
Propagation By division of root clumps, by seed, by cuttings, by simple layering.
Other taxa *R. alaternus* var. *angustifolia* has lanceolate or linear-oval toothed leaves. *R. cathartica* (Common Buckthorn), a deciduous shrub; its branches have a spiny apex and its black, globose berries are poisonous. *R. frangula* (*Frangula alnus*, Alder Buckthorn), a common deciduous shrub in damp habitats, with oval leaves.

76 RHODODENDRON ARBOREUM

Family Ericaceae.
Place of origin The Himalayas.
Description A large shrub or small tree up to 20–26 ft. (6–8 m.) in height, its oblong, lanceolate leaves are about 7 in. (18 cm.) long and 2 in. (5 cm.) across; when first unfurled they are downy and then green on the upper surface, whitish-rust color beneath. The compact, terminal inflorescence is rounded, 4¾–6 in. (12–15 cm.) in diameter, and composed of a number of bell-shaped flowers, each about 1½–2 in. (4–5 cm.) in diameter, deep pink in color with reddish-purple markings.
Cultivation It requires a strongly acid soil containing plenty of humus. Rainwater rather than tap-water should be used for watering since it contains little lime. It likes a bright or semi-shaded position but does not enjoy direct sunlight. It should be kept well away from anything that might give off reflected heat as this may cause the leaves to shrivel. It requires constant moisture during the growing period but does not react well to stagnant water, which is why the soil should be well-drained. It responds well to an occasional application of well-rotted stable manure around its base; this also helps to protect the roots.
Propagation By seed, by cuttings, by grafting, by air layering and by simple layering.
Other species The genus *Rhododendron* is huge, containing several hundred species and many more hybrids. It is beyond the scope of this book to list all those worthy of a place in the average garden, and one's local garden center or nursery should be able to advise one on what to plant.

77 RHODODENDRON SIMSII

Family Ericaceae.
Place of origin Southeast Asia.
Description A widespreading evergreen or semievergreen shrub about 3–6 ft (1–2 m.) tall, it is densely branched and its dark green, lanceolate leaves are 1½–3½ in. (4–9 cm.) in length. Its large, bell-shaped pinkish-red flowers, usually with 10 stamens but sometimes with only 8, are grouped in terminal corymbs of two or more. There are a great many hybrids, with single or double flowers in colors ranging from white through various shades of red.
Cultivation This is one of the most popular species to be cultivated commercially since it also grows well in pots or tubs. Like all species of *Rhododendron*, it requires acid, open, well-drained soil. It needs to be kept away from any direct source of heat although it likes a bright position. When grown in the ground, if the soil is not siliceous it is worth digging a fairly deep hole before planting; this should then be loosely filled with acid humus for about 20 in (0.5 m.) and the roots spread out well; the hole can then be topped up with more humus. The top surface should be renewed very three or four years. This shrub requires constant moisture.
Propagation By seed, by cuttings, by grafting, by air layering, by simple layering of the young, flexible branches.
Other species From the vast range of species of *Rhododendron*, *R. indicum* is particularly worth mentioning. It is often confused with *R. simsii* although it originates from Japan and is more hardy; its red flowers have only 5 stamens.

78 RIBES RUBRUM
Red Currant

Family Saxifragaceae.
Place of origin Europe.
Description A deciduous bushy shrub cultivated for its edible fruit. Its 3-lobed, palmate, light green leaves, borne on stems, are smooth and velvety with a dentate margin. The greenish inflorescences are gathered into short, erect racemes consisting of about 15 flowers; each flower has a pitcher-shaped calyx and a 4–5 petaled corolla with 5 stamens. The fruits develop on the flower-bearing racemes, which grow long and pendulous. The fruit is a smooth, bright red, spherical berry with a little brownish tuft at the apex; it is both acid and sweet to the taste. The plant reaches a height of 4–6 ft. (1–2 m.).
Cultivation The red currant grows well in a cool climate on deep calcareous or siliceous clayey soil. A good dressing of manure is beneficial in the spring. Careful pruning encourages fruit production; toward the end of winter all dead wood should be removed and any excess or weak branches of new growth cut out. It likes a cool position in semishade; in fairly cold areas it can be sited in full sun. This is a hardy species and frost-resistant. It needs regular watering in dry weather.
Propagation By cuttings in the spring or autumn.
Other species *R. aureum*, with yellow flowers and black fruit. *R. grossularia* (Gooseberry), with sweet yellow, edible fruit. *R. nigrum* (Black Currant), with sweet black fruit, used like red currants. *R. sanguineum* (Flowering Currant), with red flowers united in very decorative pendulous clusters and with aromatic leaves, very reliable as a spring-flowering shrub.

---

79 ROSA
Hybrid Tea Rose

Family Rosaceae.
Place of origin Cultivation in Europe, obtained by crossing a tea rose with a hybrid perpetual.
Description Small bushes of varying shapes and sizes. The plants are distinctive for their very large, fragrant, colorful blooms. The hybrid tea is the best known of the roses even though it has become widespread only relatively recently. Continual hybridizations have increased its cultivars into the thousands.
Cultivation Modern hybrids require more nourishment than the species. Because of their rapid growth, they need a monthly dressing of balanced fertilizer from April to September.

The best planting time is in early spring or autumn if bare-root varieties are used; potted plants can be put in at any time. Roses are vigorous plants, quite hardy, and actually prefer the cold to excessive heat. Most of the hybrid teas require quite severe pruning, which should be done in the spring as the buds begin to fill out. The cut should be made about ⅛ in. (3–5 mm.) above the last bud, slanting away from where the bud is emerging.
Propagation The commonest method is with softwood cuttings; these should be taken in July–August and rooted either in a sheltered position in the open or in a coldframe in light, sandy soil.

80 ROSA MOSCHATA
Musk Rose

U.S. zone 6

Family Rosaceae.
Place of origin Southern Europe, Northern India, China.
Description The musk rose belongs to a group of old-fashioned roses, known as species roses. They preceded the modern hybridizations and, fortunately, are making a welcome comeback thanks to the enthusiasm of a number of professional rose growers who have once more put them on the market.

The specific name of this rose derives from the fact that its perfume is rather like that of musk. It is a climber and its leaves consist of 5–9 oval, toothed, smooth leaflets. The flowers are pale yellow when in bud, turning white as they open. This rose has been used in the production of many modern hybrids.
Cultivation It blooms in May and June and, although it does not have a secondary flowering as do many modern species and cultivars, it is a fascinating plant. Easy to grow, it is not subject to diseases and needs no pruning if the effect desired is free and graceful; in this case, it should be given plenty of space so that it can spread without restriction. It can, however, be pruned to maintain a tidy appearance. A dressing of fertilizer is beneficial during the winter. It is fairly resistant to frost.
Propagation By grafting and cuttings.

81 ROSMARINUS OFFICINALIS
Rosemary

U.S. zone 6

Family Labiatae.
Place of origin Mediterranean region and Morocco.
Description An evergreen, suffruticose shrub, very popular as a decorative plant either in clumps or hedges but grown mainly for its aromatic qualities as a kitchen herb. It is densely branched and bushy, forming a shrub 6–7 ft. (about 2 m.) in height, with erect, woody branchlets. Its linear, almost needle-like, leaves are green on the upper surface, silvery-gray and felted on the lower; the whole plant exudes a pleasant aroma. The violet-colored flowers, which have a 2-lipped corolla with 2 purple stamens and a long, protruding style, are grouped in whorls along the branchlets. One cultivar has white flowers. This shrub is very attractive to bees. An aromatic oil used in the manufacture of some perfumes is extracted from the plant.
Cultivation It likes a warm, sunny position in well-drained, light soil. In colder climates it needs to be slightly sheltered. It is intolerant of dryness and frost but can be grown in a pot. There is a prostrate form, 'Prostratus,' that is particularly suitable for rock gardens. Rosemary makes an excellent hedge: the young plants should be placed at intervals of 20 in. (50 cm.).
Propagation By seed, by cuttings.
Other taxa *R. officinalis* 'Albus,' with white flowers. *R. officinalis* 'Blue Spire,' with dark blue flowers. *R. officinalis* 'Miss Jessup's Upright' (var. *fastigiatus*) remains in flower throughout the summer. *R. eriocalyx* (*R. lavandulaceus*), which is native to North Africa and southern Spain, has light blue flowers.

RUSCUS ACULEATUS
Butcher's Broom   **U.S. zone 7**

Family Liliaceae.
Place of origin Europe, North Africa and the Near East.
Description A small, evergreen, dioecious shrub up to about 3 ft. (1 m.) high. It is erect and bushy with striate green stems, branched toward the top; they are elastic and rigid with sessile cladodes (flat branchlets, rather like the blades of leaves, with lengthwise venation). The cladodes are green, alternate, leathery, ovate and ⅜–1⅝ in. (1–4 cm.) long with a spiny, acuminate apex. In the center of their upper surface are small scale-like leaves and tiny, greenish, insignificant male and female flowers on their respective plants. The fruits are spherical red berries, each containing 1–2 seeds, situated in the center of the cladodes, thus creating a very showy effect in the bare winter months.

In some areas butcher's broom grows wild under hedgerows, on stony, bushy hillsides and in woodlands where the plants often form part of the undergrowth.

The short, slender rhizomes smell of turpentine and are used medicinally. The early spring shoots are edible and gathered for medicinal as well as culinary purposes. It is also much grown for cutting, its red berries making an attractive display in the winter, not only brightening up the garden but also adding a splash of color in the home especially around Christmas time.

Cultivation Butcher's broom thrives on calcareous, acid, clayey soil. It is ideal as a low-growing plant for shady areas and shrubberies, under trees and as ground cover. There should always be more than one plant of each sex to ensure the production of berries. Planting is best done in about April. Put plenty of peat in each planting hole. Butcher's broom is hardy and withstands the cold but does not like dryness. Any little pieces that have died during the winter can be cut off in the spring but no further trimming is necessary.

Propagation By clump division in the spring. Reproduction by seed should be done in September but it is a very slow process.

Other taxa The hermaphrodite form of *R. aculeatus* variety is self-fertile and produces a large number of berries. *R. hypoglossum* (Double Tongue) is grown in mild climates; its cladodes are 2–2¾ in. (5–7 cm.) long and not prickly. *R. hypophyllum* is oblong, with broad cladodes 2–4 in. (5–10 cm.) long, not prickly, in whorls at the base and alternate towards the top.

83 SAMBUCUS RACEMOSA
Red-Berried Elder

Family Caprifoliaceae.

Place of origin Europe, Western Asia.

Description *S. racemosa* is a deciduous shrub from 8–12 ft. (2–4 m.) high, with hollow, pith-filled stems. It is particularly attractive in mid summer when the clusters of berries turn red. Its leaves consist of 5–7 long, oval, dentate leaflets narrowing to a long point toward the tip; they are borne on short secondary stems at the base of which are pairs of stipules in the form of nectary glands. The yellowish-white flowers are borne on short stalks in large panicles formed from numerous ramifications. Its clusters of globular, coral-red fruit remain erect when ripe rather than curving downwards. The pith of the branches is cinnamon-colored. This can be found growing wild in the shady woodlands of Europe from Spain to Bulgaria and has become naturalized farther North.

Cultivation This is an undemanding, hardy plant. It is very easy to grow and thrives in any fairly moisture-retentive, well-drained soil in a sunny or partially shaded position. It grows very quickly but has a tendency to become rather sparse; it is therefore advisable to allow new branches to grow from the base every three or four years. If standing alone, it can be trimmed back occasionally to keep it fairly low and give the best effect.

Propagation By seed, by woody cuttings.

Other species The genus *Sambucus* can be divided into two sections, the first of which includes the only herbaceous species, *S. ebulus*, which, although generally considered a weed, is quite an attractive plant, and the second, which includes the small tree or shrub species. Best known in this category, besides *S. racemosa*, is *S. nigra* (European Elder). In its tree form this can attain a height of 15–20 ft. (5–6 m.); in the wild the fruits are black when ripe. This species is very well-known for its medicinal properties. If a layer of *S. nigra* flowers is placed in a container and some rennet apples stored on top of them the apples acquire a delightfully musky fragrance. Elderflower wine (white) and Elderberry wine (red) are both produced locally in the British Isles. There are several good cultivars of *S. nigra*, including *S. nigra* 'Aurea' (Golden Elder), with yellow leaves; *S. nigra* 'Marginata,' a white-margined form. An attractive cultivar of *S. racemosa* is *S. racemosa* 'Plumosa Aurea,' with golden leaves.

84 SALVIA OFFICINALIS
Common Sage

Family Labiatae.
Place of origin Spain and western Yugoslavia.
Description A low-growing, densely branched, suffruticose shrub, growing to 2 ft. (90 cm.), cultivated for its aromatic, culinary and medicinal properties. The branchlets are compact and woody at the base. The oval, lanceolate leaves are aromatic, finely wrinkled, grayish-green on the upper surface and paler beneath; they are petiolate and more or less persistent in winter. Its violet flowers are ¾–1⅛ in. (2–3 cm.) long with a small tube and an open labiate corolla. They are grouped in whorls to form terminal spikes.
Cultivation Common sage grows wild in the fields in some regions and is widely cultivated as an aromatic plant as well as for its decorative appearance in garden borders. Bees are attracted to its flowers. It likes rich, dry, loamy soil and a warm, sunny position. The whole plant can be pruned hard in the spring. It also grows well in pots.
Winter protection The common sage needs to be protected with plastic sheeting or straw in a cold climate.
Propagation By seed, by cuttings, by division.
Other species *S. haematodes*, a biennial plant with purple flowers in the summer. *S. horminum*, an annual plant with purple floral bracts and spikes of violet flowers. *S. sclarea*, a biennial plant with light bluish-white flowers and white or pink bracts. *S. splendens* (Scarlet Sage), a subshrub with compact red flower spikes surrounded by red, pink or white bracts. *S. × superba*, a perennial herb with deep purplish-blue flowers in the summer.

85 SARCOCOCCA HUMILIS
Sweet Box

Family Buxaceae.
Place of origin China.
Description A small, evergreen shrub to 8 in. (45 cm.). Its long, shiny, dark green leaves arranged alternately on short, compact, delicate branchlets, are leathery with central venation; the tip is elongated and acuminate. The small, white, winter-blooming flowers have a lengthwise tube and are gathered into clusters at the leaf axils; their fragrance is a delight in the winter. The fleshy black berry accounts for the Greek derivation of the generic name, *sarkos*, meaning "flesh" and *kokkos*, "berry."
Cultivation This is an excellent pot plant, especially in areas where the climate is not suitable for it to survive the winter outdoors. When planted in the open, it grows well in shade but likes open, moist soil.
Winter protection It should be protected with plastic sheeting during prolonged spells of extremely cold weather or, if in pots, put under cover.
Propagation By seed, by cuttings, by division.
Other species *S. confusa* has a bushy habit, to 6 ft. (2 m.); fruits black. *S. ruscifolia*, from China, has small clusters of fragrant white flowers and round red fruits.

86 SENECIO LAXIFOLIUS

Family Compositae.
Place of origin New Zealand.
Description A very decorative evergreen bushy shrub attaining a height of 6–10 ft. (2–3 m.). Its daisy-like flowers are bright yellow and its leaves are white-felted underneath. It is a useful hedging plant, being both effective and unusual. Its fruit is distinguished by a pappus consisting of very fine hairs of equal length. It was undoubtedly this beard-like feature, which is common to all the species of the genus, that caused the first-century Roman naturalist, Pliny the Elder, to give these plants the generic name of *Senecio*, from the Latin *senex*, "old man."
Cultivation It is ideal for exposed coastal areas. It prefers sandy, well-drained soil enriched with well-rotted garden humus or manure. The best time for planting is in the spring or autumn. Each planting hole should be filled with peat. To create a hedge, the young plants should be placed at intervals of 18 in. (45 cm.). A dressing of humus or well-rotted manure should be put over the roots in April. A further dressing of a general fertilizer can also be given in the summer to stimulate vigorous growth. Regular deadheading is essential to encourage continuous flowering. Any straggly branches in a hedge can be trimmed into shape in April.
Propagation By softwood cuttings, 2¾–4 in. (7–10 cm.) long, in July–September.

87 SOLANUM SODOMEUM
Apple of Sodom

Family Solanaceae.
Place of origin South Africa (Cape of Good Hope).
Description This densely branched, perennial shrub, reaching a height of 10 ft. (3 m.) is quite common in hot, dry regions and is particularly recognizable by its distinctive, more or less fleshy fruits. These take the form of poisonous yellow berries of about ¾–1¼ in. (2–3 cm.) diameter. The branches are covered with yellow spines and the leaves are deeply lobate, prickly and covered with starry hairs. The flowers are violet with a prickly calyx.
Cultivation *S. sodomeum* grows freely in uncultivated areas, especially near the sea. Its needs are minimal provided that the climate is temperate-hot. It grows in any soil, even if it is arid, and tolerates dryness well.
Propagation By seed.

88 SPARTIUM JUNCEUM
Spanish Broom

U.S. zone 7

Family Leguminosae.
Place of origin Southern Europe, North Africa, Anatolia, the Crimea and western Syria.
Description A hardy shrub that grows wild in the Mediterranean region along the coast, on lakesides, in woodlands and on sunny slopes. It has rush-like, cylindridal, erect branches attaining a height of about 6–12 ft. (2–4 m.). Its large, fragrant papilionaceous flowers, arranged in loose terminal racemes, are supported by a 5-lobed calyx; the golden-yellow corolla has a long upper petal. Its fruit is a narrow, linear pod that is at first pubescent, then becomes black and smooth as it ripens.
Cultivation Ideal for producing splashes of color. This plant does not object to poor soil but likes a warm, sunny position. To encourage more abundant flowering and to prevent plants from becoming overgrown and straggly, the previous year's branches can be cut out in March before the flowers appear on the current year's growth. A dressing of manure in the spring is beneficial.
Propagation By seed in the spring; flowering occurs in the following year.

---

89 SPIRAEA JAPONICA
(syn. *S. callosa*)
Japanese Spiraea

U.S. zone 6

Family Rosaceae.
Place of origin Japan.
Description A deciduous, erect, twiggy shrub with a slightly untidy habit. It reaches a height of 3–6½ ft. (1–2 m.). Its dark green, dentate, narrowly oval leaves are 2¾–4 in. (7–10 cm.) long, 1–1½ in. (2.5–4 cm.) across and glaucous on the lower surface. The bark on the stems is glossy. The inflorescences are grouped in flat, dense, branched corymbs carried on the current year's branches. The tiny flowers of which the corymbs are composed are deep reddish-pink. It is suitable for making an unusual hedge and is particularly attractive when growing by water, where the reflection of its flowering branches can double its decorative impact.
Cultivation It is hardy in the British Isles and withstands quite hard winters and the polluted air of cities. *S. japonica* can be planted at any time in spring or autumn. If the ground is poor, a good supply of peat should be worked in around the root system. If the ground is too porous, the roots should be mulched with humus or well-rotted manure. The dead heads should be removed regularly. Prune out some of the old branches in the spring so these do not become too spindly.
Propagation By seed, by softwood cuttings, by simple layering or by separating the suckers that spring from the base.
Other species *S. thunbergii*, the earliest-flowering species, flowering March–April.

90 SYMPHORICARPOS ALBUS

(syn. *S. racemosus*)
Snowberry   **U.S. zone 4**

Family Caprifoliaceae.

Place of origin North America.

Description An ornamental, deciduous shrub of great elegance. It attains a height of 4½–6½ ft. (1½–2 m.) and an overall width of about 6½–9 ft. (2–2½ m.). The opposite, oval leaves are entire or lobate, sometimes with a grayish underside, and borne on short stalks. The small flowers, in clusters of 1–3, are borne on short stems, and are bell-shaped, velvety on the inside and tinged with pink on the outside. Flowering June–July.

S. albus is distinguishable from other species because the stamens, like the style, do not extend beyond the edge of the corolla and are thus embedded. The flowers are very attractive to bees. Its waxy white berries are formed in clusters on the branches and it is for this reason that the generic name *Symphoricarpos* derives from the Greek *karpos* and *symphorein* meaning "berries borne together." These fruits remain on the branches most of the winter if the birds leave them alone.

Cultivation It is ideal for a poor, windy terrain and tolerates lime. It is especially suitable for low hedges or as ground cover. It is cold-resistant and can be planted in good weather in spring or autumn. In a hedge the young plants should be placed at intervals of 24 in. (60 cm.). This shrub requires little attention but the roots should be mulched in the spring if the ground is too loose and porous. No regular pruning is necessary but any damaged or unsightly branches should be removed in spring. In older plants the old wood should be thinned out from the center. Hedges can be trimmed toward the end of winter or beginning of spring.

Propagation It propagates easily by removing some of the numerous suckers that spring from the base; the little plants that result can be planted out between March and April. Softwood cuttings about 2¾–4 in. (7–10 cm.) long, with a heel, can also be taken in July–September.

Other species *S. occidentalis* (Wolfberry), which is early flowering, even before *S. albus*. Its flowers form dense spikes with the style and stamens projecting beyond the edge of the corolla, the inside of the corolla being bearded. *S. orbiculatus*, introduced into Europe in 1732. Its leaves are pubescent on the underside and the small red and yellow flowers are grouped in clusters in the axils of all the leaves; the corolla, slightly bearded on the inside, flares out like a bell and its tube is much shorter than its lobes; its berries are no larger than juniper berries. *S. microphyllus*, with whitish-pink berries, is not a widely grown species because it is not very hardy.

91 SYRINGA VULGARIS
Common Lilac

Family Oleaceae.
Place of origin Eastern Europe.
Description An ornamental deciduous shrub or small tree that can attain a height of 23 ft. (7 m.); it is grown for its hardiness and for its elegant, fragrant flowers. The woody stems are densely branched. Its ovate, cordate leaves are smooth and delicate, up to 4 in. (10 cm.) long, with fine prominent venation. Its purple, lilac, blue, pink, red or white flowers are grouped in erect, conical, terminal panicles. The fruit consists of a bivalved capsule.
Cultivation Lilac grows in any soil but has a preference for clayey, damp ground. It likes sun in a cold climate and shade in a warm climate. It is very hardy. A dressing of manure in the spring is beneficial. Lilac should be pruned at the end of the flowering season to remove the dead flowers and any damaged or inactive branches; root and stem suckers should be removed whenever they appear since they drain the plant of strength. Mildew on the foliage in the summer is unsightly but not serious.
Propagation By seed, by cuttings, by division of root shoots, by air layering, by grafting.
Other taxa *S. emodi*, with panicles of violet flowers. *S. microphylla*, (Littleleaf Lilac), a low-growing shrub, to about 5 ft. (2 m.) with pink flowers and a long flowering period. *S. josikaea*, (Hungarian Lilac), with clusters of purple flowers with little scent. *S. × persica*, (Persian Lilac), with lanceolate leaves. *S. reflexa*, with long, pendulous clusters of pink flowers. *S. sweginzowii*, with long clusters of very fragrant pink flowers.

---

92 TAMARIX TETRANDRA
Tamarisk

Family Tamaricaceae.
Place of origin Southern Europe and Asia Minor.
Description A deciduous shrub with an untidy head, it reaches a height of 20 ft. (6 m.). It is grown as an ornamental plant, especially for its elegant, dainty inflorescences. The bark of its stems is dark. The small, pale green leaves are scale-like. Its tiny, pale pink flowers are arranged on long, slim spikes; they have 4 stamens and it is from this characteristic that the species derives its name. It is particularly well-suited to a mild climate, especially near the sea or in desert areas, where it helps to prevent the sand drifting.
Cultivation The tamarisk is hardy and able to withstand the cold in a mild climate. It is a lime-hater but likes a sandy soil. It is resistant to the wind. It can be pruned, quite hard if necessary, after flowering to remove any weak and straggly branches.
Propagation By cuttings in the autumn.
Other species *T. africana*, with slightly larger floral spikes. *T. anglica*, a suitable shrub for hedging or to form individual clumps. *T. gallica*, a tall shrub with erect branches and clusters of pink flowers. *T. hispida*, a shrub with hairy branches and leaves, its deep pink flowers appear rather late. *T. ramosissima (T. pentandra)*, with small white and pink flowers. *T. parviflora* flowers on old wood and is light pink.

93 ULEX EUROPAEUS
Gorse, Furze, Whin

Family Leguminosae.

Place of origin Europe.

Description An evergreen shrub, 6–10 ft. (2–3 m.) high, that grows wild in stony, acid terrain, on moorlands and heaths. It looks – and is – extremely hardy. Its furrowed branches are rigid and crowded close together, bearing a few leaves and long spines. Its small, tripartite, needle-like leaves are widely spaced, alternating with the spines, which are, in fact, small branches or pointed leaf stalks. The yellow, scented flowers, about ¾ in. (2 cm.) long, have a hairy calyx and papilionaceous corolla; they grow singly in the leaf axils. The fruit is a short, hairy, well-filled legume that bursts and scatters the seeds when ripe.

Cultivation Gorse needs poor, calcareous, fairly dry soil. It thrives in mild and warm climates but it can be damaged by frost. It survives in a windy position but likes the sun. It is a useful plant for dry gardens and makes a good hedge. It does not tolerate being transplanted or pruned, although hedges can be lightly trimmed.

Propagation Sow directly into the growing position in the spring or autumn to avoid transplanting; cuttings can be taken in July.

Other species *U. gallii*, a low-growing, evergreen, densely spiny shrub that flowers in late summer. *U. minor (U. nanus)*, a dwarf evergreen shrub that produces small yellow flowers in the autumn. *U. parviflorus*, which grows wild in the siliceous soil of southwest Europe, has small flowers and sturdier spines than other species.

---

94 VITEX AGNUS-CASTUS
Chaste Tree

Family Verbenaceae.

Place of origin Mediterranean region and southwest and central Asia.

Description An aromatic deciduous shrub with a bushy, dense habit, attaining a height of 10–13 ft. (3–4 m.). Its branches are long and slender with opposite, petiolate leaves; they consist of 5–7 narrow, lanceolate leaflets, greenish-gray on the upper surface and white beneath. The inflorescences form long, erect, narrow, terminal racemes. The flowers have a 5-toothed calyx, a small violet corolla opening out into 5 lobes with 4 stamens and a long style. The fruit is a small 4-lobed, reddish-black drupe.

The chaste tree was known in antiquity, the specific name referring to chastity – both *agnos*, in Greek, and *castus* in Latin, mean "chaste." It grows wild by river beds, on wasteland and, mainly in Mediterranean regions, along the coast.

Cultivation The chaste tree grows well in any type of soil provided that it is damp. It likes a warm, sunny position. It is well-suited for hedging, because it is scented, colorful and forms a good windbreak. It should be hard-pruned in the spring.

Propagation By seed, by cuttings.

Other taxa *V. negundo*, originally from southeast Asia, a smaller shrub with erect, violet racemes. *V. agnus-castus* forma *alba*, flowers white.

VIBURNUM OPULUS
Guelder Rose

Family Caprifoliaceae.

Place of origin Europe, northwest Africa, Asia Minor, Caucasus and parts of central Asia.

Description A deciduous shrub with a graceful head, its autumn foliage and clusters of scarlet fruits are very decorative. It has an erect habit, attains a height of 15 ft. (5 m.), and has erect branches. The opposite, dark green leaves, are up to 4 in. (10 cm.) long and divided into 3–5 dentate lobes, smooth on the upper surface and downy beneath. They shade into wonderful colors in the autumn. The white inflorescences are gathered into flat cymes borne on long peduncles. The 5-lobed, broad, external flowers are sterile and attract insects while the central bell-shaped flowers are fertile. Its red, rounded drupes, each of which contains a single seed, are juicy and glossy but poisonous; they remain on the plant for a long time. This viburnum grows wild by streams, in hedgerows and woodlands; it is not a long-lived plant.

Cultivation It requires calcareous, moist, well-drained, deep soil. Its favorite position is in semishade. It can be planted in late winter and benefits from a dressing of manure and a good mulching every spring. It can safely be hard-pruned if it needs to be given a new lease of life or to remove parts damaged by frost.

Propagation By seed, by grafting, by simple layering, by cuttings in the summer.

Other taxa *V. opulus* 'Nanum,' a bush shrub about 3 ft. (1 m.) high. *V. opulus* 'Roseum' (*V. opulus* 'Sterile,' Snowball Tree), with spherical, sterile inflorescences. *V.* × *burkwoodii*, with fragrant pink to white flowers. *V.* × *carlcephalum*, with fragrant, small, white flowers in rounded heads 5 in. (12 cm.) across. *V. carlesii*, popular because of its very fragrant flowers. *V. farreri* (*V. fragrans*), another fragrant species, the corymbs of pink and white flowers appearing before the leaves. *V. lantana*, with ovate leaves and fruits that turn from red to black. *V. plicatum* forma *plicatum*, with white flowers in round balls. *V. plicatum* forma *tomentosum, (V. tomentosum)*, with broad, flat inflorescences that have showy external sterile flowers; the red fruits turn black as they ripen. One of the very best viburnums. *V. rhytidophyllum*, with long, rugose, evergreen leaves and yellowish white flowers in flat clusters; *V. setigerum* 'Aurantiacum', with beautiful orange berries. *V. sieboldii*, growing to 10 ft. (3 m.) and very hardy, with creamy white flowers in flat clusters. *V. tinus* 'Laurustinus' an evergreen shrub, which flowers in winter.

96 WEIGELA FLORIDA

Family Caprifoliaceae.
Place of origin China, Korea
Description A deciduous shrub about 9 ft. (3 m.) tall. Its elliptic, ovate leaves are 2–4 in. (5–10 cm.) long and smooth on the upper surface. The flowers have a funnel-shaped corolla, pink outside and white inside; it grows close to the calyx, which widens out evenly into 5 lobes; the sepals are detached, for part of their length, from the calyx. The name of the genus is dedicated to the 19th-century German botanist Christian von Weigel (1748–1831).
Cultivation A hardy plant, it grows well in either full sun or semishade. It likes peaty or well-manured, moist soil and is lime-tolerant. When pruning, care should be taken not to spoil the delicate, slender appearance of the plant: remove only the branches that have already flowered, those that are crowding the new shoots and any old branches that do not bear flowers.
Propagation By woody cuttings in the autumn, by softwood cuttings in the summer.
Other species *W. coraeensis*, from Japan, with rigid, smooth branches and white or pink flowers. *W. floribunda*, also from Japan, with hairy, weeping branches and numerous small, deep pink flowers. *W. japonica*, with hairy leaves and red flowers. *W. middendorffiana*, with yellow and pink flowers.

97 YUCCA RECURVIFOLIA

Family Liliaceae.
Place of origin Southeastern United States.
Description An evergreen shrub with a main stem that becomes woody with time. In a warm climate it can reach a height of nearly 6 ft. (2 m.) and a breadth of about 6½ ft–7 ft. (2–2½ m.). Its large leaves, in rosette form, are leathery, grayish-green and up to about 3 ft. (90 cm.) in length; they spring from the ground when the plant is young but later emerge from the top of the short main stem and end in a very sharp spine. The panicles of creamy-white flowers are borne on scapes up to 3 ft. (90 cm.) high. This species seldom flowers and certainly not before the main stem is about 2 ft. (60 cm.) tall.
Cultivation *Y. recurvifolia* lives and thrives for a reasonable length of time in ordinary well-drained garden soil as well as on the seashore and among sand dunes exposed to salt-laden winds. It even lives in poor soil and tolerates shallow soil on limestone. It grows well in the sun and withstands the cold quite well. It should be planted in April or October.
Propagation By detaching the offshoots from the base, preferably in the spring but also in the summer or autumn. If the offshoots are rather small, it is advisable to bring them on in a nursery bed.
Other species *Y. filamentosa* (Adam's Needle), has no main stem; its leaves have numerous curly white filaments along their edges. *Y. glauca*, with glaucous leaves. *Y. whipplei*, with greenish-white, scented flowers borne on a scape that can attain a height of 10–13 ft. (3–4 m.).

98 ACACIA DEALBATA

Family Leguminosae.

Place of origin Tasmania and Australia.

Description *A. dealbata* is one of the most widely grown acacias in temperate climates and the most in demand from florists.

In its native habitat, it can grow to 100 ft. (32 m.), but is smaller in cultivation and in some places where it has become naturalized its trunk can achieve a circumference of 10 ft. (3 m.). It is evergreen and has a luxuriant, tousled appearance. The leaves are very elegant; they are 2¾–4¾ in. (7–12 cm.) long, bipinnate and consist of 15–20 segments each of which is made up of 30–50 silvery-gray, feathery leaflets. The deep yellow, very fragrant flowers, are borne in panicles 2¾–4 in. (7–10 cm.) long; the distinctive globose heads are formed by masses of long-stalked stamens crowded together spherically.

Cultivation A mixture of acid humus and sand with clay and loam is required. The richer the soil, the better the plant will thrive, but it also grows well in poor soil. Mimosa is not particularly hardy and prefers a sheltered position in full sun, against a wall in areas where the climate is less than mild in the winter. It needs to be kept well-watered in dry weather. It should be pruned after flowering.

Winter protection In areas where the winter is hard *A. dealbata* needs to be protected during the coldest months by some sort of removable covering such as burlap or plastic sheeting. In milder climates it can be sited with greater freedom, without the protection of a wall.

Propagation By seed or by semihardwood cuttings.

Other species *A. armata* (Kangaroo Thorn), spiny with rich yellow flowers, also requires a temperate climate. *A. longifolia*, with bright yellow flowers borne in cylindrical spikes about 1⅜ in. (3.5 cm.) long. *A. farnesiana*, widespread in tropical countries, is deciduous, spiny and has scented orange-yellow flowers. It cannot stand the cold and therefore will need protection.

99 ACER NEGUNDO
Box Elder

Family Aceraceae.
Place of origin North America.
Description A quick-growing but short-lived deciduous tree, it grows to a height of 30–60 ft. (10–20 m.). It has an untidy head and is densely branched. The leaves, unlike those of other *Acer* species, are pinnate, 6–12 in. (15–30 cm.) long, consisting of 3–7 light green, oval leaflets with a dentate margin. Its dioecious, greenish flowers are insignificant and appear before the leaves. The male flowers are gathered into erect, pedunculate inflorescences and the females are in pendulous racemes. The fruits are samaras, or "keys," with divergent, narrow, incurving brown wings that remain on the trees after the leaves have fallen.
Cultivation It requires damp, preferably clayey soil, and a position in full sun. It is tolerant of changes in climate but does not like dryness or high winds.
Propagation By seed, by grafting, or by cuttings.
Other taxa *A. negundo* 'Variegatum,' with white-edged leaves. *A. negundo* 'Aureo-Marginatum,' with yellow-edged leaves. *A. negundo* var. *californicum*, this is a subspecies with downy leaves. *A. palmatum* (Japanese Maple), a shrub or small tree up to 20 ft. (7 m.) in cultivation. Leaves palmately 5- or 7-lobed, green, becoming bronzed in autumn. Native to Japan, China and Korea. This species has produced a large range of forms and cultivars, differing in leaf shape and color.

---

100 ALBIZIA JULIBRISSIN
Pink Siris, Silk Tree

Family Leguminosae.
Place of origin Near East.
Description A deciduous tree attaining a height of 33 ft. (10 m.) with a broad, expansive head due to its spreading, almost horizontal branches and pendulous branchlets. Its little pink flowers, rather like tiny powderpuffs, make this a particularly decorative tree. The frondlike, bipinnate leaves are 6–12 in. (15–30 cm.) long, and consist of 6–12 pinnae bearing up to 30 pairs of oblong, ciliate leaflets, giving the plant a light, delicate appearance. The scented flowers are grouped in terminal racemose clusters. Numerous showy pink and white thread-like stamens emerge from the corollas.
    The fruit is an undulate, narrow, greenish pod on a long stalk; it is transparent at first, becoming dry as it ripens. The generic name derives from that of the Florentine nobleman Filippo degli Albizzi who imported it from Constantinople in the middle of the 18th century. The specific name is Iranian.
Cultivation This tree is fairly hardy and in a temperate climate is able to tolerate short periods of cold and frost as long as these are not too intense. It does not mind dryness and likes a sunny position. It is lime-hating but grows in poor or sandy soil.
Propagation By seed.
Other taxa *A. julibrissin* 'Rosea'; this summer-flowering plant is smaller, more cold-resistant and its flowers are a deeper pink. *A. lebbek*, with greenish-white or brownish flowers and longer leaflets. *A. lophanta*, from Australia, bears long, greenish-yellow flat racemes of flowers.

ARBUTUS UNEDO
Strawberry Tree   **U.S. zone 9**

Family Ericaceae.

Place of origin The Mediterranean region and southwest Ireland.

Description A small tree, also growing as a shrub in the wild, attaining a height of up to 30 ft. (12 m.). It is evergreen and has a dense, rounded head. Its trunk is often branched from the base, from which spring numerous suckers. The branches are erect, pinkish and velvety when young, becoming darker and scaly with age. Its alternate, obovate or lanceolate, dark green leaves are 2–3¼ in. (5–8 cm.) long; they are leathery and glossy. The small flowers are white or pink and grouped in dense pendulous, panicles; they have an urn-shaped corolla, which is divided into 5 teeth and supported by the 5 short lobes of the calyx. The fruit is a sweet, edible, globose, red berry, ⅜–¾ in. (1–2 cm.) across, with a granular surface and pale, juicy pulp.

The strawberry tree is grown in mild climates for its crowded, glossy crown, which provides shade, for the attractive, pendulous flowers, and for the fruits, which can be used to make alcoholic drinks. The flowers appear in the autumn or at the beginning of winter when the previous year's fruit is ripe, resulting in a striking display in three colors. Birds are gluttons for the fruits and help to disseminate the seeds. It is a gregarious plant, typical of the Mediterranean "maquis," where it mixes happily with other species such as the cork tree, myrtle, laurel, and the holm or evergreen oak.

Cultivation The strawberry tree is a hardy, heat-loving plant, resistant to dryness and a marine climate. It rarely grows in calcareous soil but prefers siliceous, sandy, arid ground provided that it is not too acid. It is a slow grower. It can survive fire by throwing up suckers and is an ideal plant for colonization and reforestation. It needs to be in full sun or semishade. It can be grown in a pot. It does not like long periods of intense cold. If pruning is necessary, this should be done in April.

Winter protection Small plants should be sheltered with plastic sheeting and in cold areas any that are in pots should be put under cover.

Propagation By air layering, by simple layering, by cuttings, by seed (this is a slow method), by division of the suckers.

Other species *A. andrachne*, which has broader leaves with an entire margin when adult; it blooms in the spring in erect inflorescences and has smaller, orange fruits. *A. × andrachnoides*, a natural hybrid between the two previous species; it is more resistant to the cold and has a spectacular reddish bark. *A. menziesii* (Madrone), originating from North America, can reach a height of nearly 100 ft. (30 m.); its fruit is usable in the same way as that of *A. unedo*.

102 CAMELLIA JAPONICA
Common Camellia

Family Theaceae.
Place of origin Japan, Korean archipelago, Liu Kiu Islands.
Description The first species of camellia to have been introduced into Europe (1792) and the United States (1797) it was very popular in the 19th century and is still the species most frequently seen in European and American gardens. Named for the 17th-century Moravian Jesuit and pharmacist Georg Kamel.

A small, slow-growing, evergreen tree or shrub that reaches a height of 40 ft. (14 m.), it has an expansive, broad head and branches springing from the base; its habit is sometimes bushy. The alternate, oval leaves are leathery, a deep glossy green on the upper surface and lighter beneath. The flowers are up to 5 in. (13 cm.) across and supported by 5 green sepals with pinkish-white petals; the cultivars are also to be found in pink and red with numerous stamens. They are very delicate and easily damaged by high wind and heavy rain. The fruit consists of a round, woody capsule, depressed into 3 lengthwise grooves.
Cultivation It needs a well-drained, acid soil that is kept well-fertilized and rich in humus. It likes a bright position, sheltered from the wind, but should not be in full sun in a warm climate. It also grows well in a pot. It should be transplanted when in flower as the new shoots begin to appear immediately after flowering.
Propagation By grafting, by cuttings, by air layering, by seed.
Other species *C. cuspidata*, very hardy. *C. reticulata*, a delicate plant with deep pink flowers. *C. sasanqua*, with smaller leaves, gray below, has small, slightly scented pink flowers. *C. sinensis* (Tea Plant), has white flowers and is not hardy.

103 CERCIS SILIQUASTRUM
Judas Tree

Family Leguminosae.
Place of origin Eastern Mediterranean region and the Near East.
Description A deciduous tree that can attain a height of 33 ft. (10 m.), the Judas tree is densely branched and has a graceful, spreading habit. It is grown for its elegant foliage and showy springtime blossom. It is said to be the tree from which Judas hanged himself, the pink flowers being no doubt symbolic of blood. Its rounded, smooth, kidney-shaped leaves are about 4 in. (10 cm.) across and petiolate; they are bright green on the upper surface and paler beneath. The flowers, which emerge in clusters before the leaves, spring directly from the bark of the bare branches; they are bright pink and pea-like. The fruits are brown, drooping pods that persist during the winter.
Cultivation The Judas tree grows in any kind of soil provided that it is moist. It needs a warm, sunny position and is not very frost-resistant. If it becomes damaged for any reason, it can be pruned hard.
Winter protection Young plants should be protected from hard, prolonged frost.
Propagation By seed, transplanting the young plant after two years.
Other species *C. chinensis* (Chinese Redbud), originally from China. *C. occidentalis* (Western Redbud), a tree that needs a favorable, mild climate. *C. racemosa* from China, has large rose-colored racemes.

104 CITRUS AURANTIUM
Seville Orange, Bitter Orange

U.S. zone 9

Family Rutaceae.
Place of origin Southeast Asia. It was introduced into Europe in the 12th century by the Arabs.
Description An evergreen tree that can attain a height of 20 ft. (6 m.), it has a dome-shaped crown with spiny branches. It throws up suckers freely. Its large, alternate, coriaceous leaves are oval to elliptic with an alate petiole. The white, scented flowers are either gathered into corymbs or isolated. The spherical fruits, with rough skin, turn a brilliant shade of orange when ripe. The sour, very bitter pulp contains a number of seeds. Apart from being decorative, the bitter orange is used to make marmalade and medicinal products. It is also used as stock on which other *Citrus* species are grafted. In addition, essences are obtained from the leaves, unripe fruit and flowers; these are used in the making of perfumes and soap.
Cultivation It likes loose, open soil with frequent watering. It is the hardiest of the citruses and withstands winter temperatures, down to 32°F (0°C) but cannot stand frost. It is recommended not only for its decorative value in a garden but also because it requires less attention than the other citruses. In countries where the climate is mild, it is not uncommon to see bitter orange trees, laden with fruit, lining avenues and promenades.
Winter protection The trees should be protected with straw matting or plastic sheeting during spells of severe winter weather. They need conservatory treatment in the British Isles.
Propagation By seed from November to March after having soaked the seeds in water for some time.

---

105 CITRUS AURANTIUM subsp. BERGAMIA
(syn. *C. bergamia*)
Bergamot

U.S. zone 10

Family Rutaceae.
Place of origin China.
Description A fairly small tree from 10 to 16½ ft. (3–5 m.) high with a compact crown and low branches. Its leathery, elongated-ovate leaves are slightly bullate when mature; they are dark green on the upper surface and pale green beneath. The scented white flowers grow either singly or grouped into corymbs. The fruits may be spherical, slightly flattened at top and bottom, or oblong; their skin varies in thickness according to the cultivar; they are pale yellow when ripe and have acidulous pulp. An essence is extracted from the skin, known as essence of bergamot, which is used in the making of better quality perfumes, especially eau de cologne, and to flavor confectionery, tobacco and liqueurs. The essence also has antiseptic and wound-healing properties. Special essences are also obtained from the flowers and leaves. The residual pulp that remains after the essences have been extracted from the fruit is used in cattle fodder.
Cultivation The bergamot likes loose, open soil. It needs frequent watering and can survive only in a warm climate; otherwise it has to be grown in a pot and removed to the protection of a greenhouse during the winter.
Winter protection Protective measures must be taken wherever the winter climate is severe. Bergamot is not hardy.
Propagation By grafting on to bitter orange stock.

106 CITRUS LIMON
Lemon

Family Rutaceae.
Place of origin India.
Description A small evergreen tree, attaining a height of 20 ft. (6 m.), with an irregular head. The new season's shoots are violet. The alternate, ovate-lanceolate leaves have spiny stipules and leaf-like wings on the stalk. Its sweetly scented flowers are white, tinged with purplish-violet, springing from the leaf axils either singly or in pairs. The most important florescence is in April–May and gives rise to the winter fruit crop; the September florescence leads to the "summer lemons" of June–August. The trees begin to bear fruit in their fourth or fifth years, the crop continuing to increase until they are about 15 years old. The fruits are oval or elliptic with an umbo at one end. The golden-yellow skin of the fruit may be rough or smooth, rich in essential oils – a common feature, of many species of *Citrus* – with bitter, acidulous pulp, although some cultivars have sweet pulp. On average, the tree lives for about 80 years.

The juice of the fruit is used for flavoring soft drinks and confectionery and medicinally as a valuable source of vitamin C for preventing colds. Perhaps no other fruit has received so much praise, beginning in the 5th century B.C. when Theophrastus, the Greek philosopher, cited it as an antidote to poison. The peel of the lemon, too, contains valuable oils used in making perfumes and as an aid to digestion.

Cultivation *C. limon* cannot tolerate frost and needs a sunny position with loose, well-drained, well-fertilized soil. It does not like being transplanted; care should be taken to keep the root ball intact when moving a young tree. The plants require little watering in winter but a great deal in spring and summer. Like all *Citrus* trees, it needs about 2 pounds of nitrogen fertilizer, divided into several equal applications, per year.

Winter protection The lemon tree should be protected wherever the winter temperature falls below 45–47°F (7–8°C). It needs conservatory treatment in the British Isles.

Propagation By seed, by grafting on to stock, by grafting on to a dormant bud in a nursery bed.

107 CITRUS × PARADISI
Grapefruit

U.S. zone 10

Family Rutaceae.

Place of origin Presumably derived from the hybridization of *C. maxima* and originating from the West Indies.

Description An evergreen tree, attaining a height of 40 ft. (12 m.), with a dense, dome-shaped crown 26–29 ft. (8–9 m.) in diameter. Its dark green, ovate, leaves are borne on a slightly winged stalk and a flexible spine springs from the leaf axils. The white flowers grow either singly or in axillary racemes. Its fruit is quite large and round, often slightly flattened on the top and bottom, with light yellow skin and pulp, the latter being acidulous and bitter. Apart from being eaten raw, the fruit is used to make marmalade and pectin, and essential oils are obtained from the skin; the waste material is used in cattle fodder.

Cultivation This species is very sensitive to the cold and should be grown in a warm, sheltered position. It likes loose soil and needs to be kept well-watered in the summer. In colder climates it requires conservatory treatment.

Winter protection Protection is necessary whenever freezing temperatures are likely.

Propagation By grafting on to the bitter orange or, in cooler areas, on to *Poncirus trifoliata*.

---

108 CITRUS SINENSIS
Sweet Orange

U.S. zone 9

Family Rutaceae.

Place of origin Asia.

Description An evergreen tree about 26–33 ft. (8–10 m.) in height. It has a compact form, either conical or umbrella-shaped, and is about 13–16 ft. (4–5 m.) across. The branches sometimes have small spines. Its dark green leaves are ovate or ovate-elliptic in shape and borne on a slightly winged stalk. Its white, heavily scented flowers are grouped in axillary racemes. Its fruits have a yellowish-orange skin when ripe and a juicy pulp rich in sugars and organic acids.

Cultivation The orange tree grows well in temperate-warm climates in loose soil of average quality. It needs an annual dressing of fertilizer and regular, overall watering in the summer. It is very sensitive to sudden changes in temperature, both up and down.

Winter protection The orange tree requires plenty of protection whenever it is in anything but a warm temperate atmosphere.

CORNUS MAS
Cornelian Cherry

Family Cornaceae.

Place of origin Europe.

Description A sturdy, hardy small tree. It prefers calcareous, fairly dry, compact soil; in the wild it grows singly or in small groups on sunny hillsides and slopes, in hedgerows and in broadleaved woodlands on plains and hills up to an altitude of about 4,200 ft. (1,300 m.).

The cornelian cherry is a deciduous tree, attaining a height of 16–26 ft. (5–8 m.). Its brown and gray bark flakes off toward the base of the bole from which spring numerous shoots. Its leaves are opposite, oval and acuminate. The fragrant flowers appear early, in clusters of yellow on the bare branches, each one held by 4 greenish external bracts; they are very small, their corolla consisting of 4 smooth petals and 4 stamens. Its early flowering makes this small tree easy to recognize among other trees and shrubs. The fruits are oblong, pendulous berries about ⅜–¾ in. (1–2 cm.) long; they become brilliantly red and glossy when ripe. Each berry contains a very hard, ellipsoidal nut.

Cornelian cherries have an acid but pleasant taste, and are particularly sought by birds.

The wood, which is hard and durable but springy, was used by the Romans to make javelins. It was also used to make the spokes of wheels, gearwheel teeth for olive presses and mills, utensil handles, ladder rungs etc.

Cultivation This plant can withstand cold and lives for a long time, often growing rapidly for about its first 20 years. It prefers to be sited in full sun since it loves the heat and is tolerant of dryness. It grows in any type of soil, even clay, but benefits from a good dressing of humus after it has been transplanted. It can be trimmed to maintain a good shape or made into a hedge.

The cornelian cherry is grown for its ornamental quality as a small tree, bush, hedge or over a pergola and for its early bloom, autumnal colors and edible fruit, which attract birds to the garden. The berries can be used in making jams and sauces or preserved in brine. At one time, lamp oil was extracted from the hard seeds.

Propagation By seed and by cuttings.

Other species *C. florida* (Flowering Dogwood), a small tree to 20 ft. (7 m.) in cultivation, showy white bracts in May. *C. kousa*, to 20 ft. (7 m.), bushy habit, 4 creamy white bracts, fleshy, strawberry-like red fruit. *C. macrophylla*, a tree 30–50 ft. (10–16 m.) in height. Flowers yellowish-white. Fruits globose, blue when ripe. *C. nuttallii* (Pacific Dogwood), with magnificent large white showy bracts.

Family   Rosaceae.

Place of origin   Unknown, probably Near East and central Asia.

Description   A small deciduous, rather twisted, tree with short, outstretched branches attaining a height of 16–26 ft. (5–8 m.). It is a slow grower. The tough, alternate leaves are oval-elliptic and entire, about 4 in. (10 cm.) long, dark green and smooth on the upper surface, and gray with thick down on the underside. The large, pink or white, sweetly scented flowers grow singly; they are about 2 in. (5 cm.) across, with 5 petals each ¾ in. (2 cm.) long, numerous stamens and a persistent calyx.

The quince fruit, which has an aromatic perfume, is like a large, golden-yellow apple elongated to a pear shape and covered with fine down; it stays on the tree into autumn, even after the leaves have fallen.

In spite of their hard, woody consistency, quinces have several uses. They are often used to perfume cupboards and drawers and, when cooked, they can be used to make quince jam and jelly as well as liqueurs. Their sharp, astringent flavor has also been exploited for medicinal purposes.

The quince was known to the Greeks who named it for the ancient Cretan city of Cydonia. It has now become naturalized throughout Europe. In warm regions it grows wild, has a shrubby habit and bears small fruit. It has been cultivated since antiquity for its scented fruits. These were the "golden apples" used in ancient traditional medicines and ceremonials, and offered to the gods in ancient Greek religious and nuptial rites as symbols of love and fertility.

Cultivation   The quince tree likes a cool climate with open, non calcareous, clayey soil, and needs to be kept moist and, most important, fertile because the roots are quite shallow. The tree benefits from having all suckers and side shoots removed. The quince is not a difficult tree to grow provided that it is exposed to the sun and sheltered from cold winds. The flowers come into bud quite late, therefore it is not damaged by spring frosts. To get a good fruit crop, however, it is essential that the tree is well-sited and it should be pruned every year, given plenty of fertilizer or manure and treated with an antiparasitic substance every winter.

Propagation   By cuttings, by grafting on to a pear tree, by removing the side shoots from the trunk and rooting them.

Other taxa   Cultivars to grow for fruit: 'Orange' is the oldest and gives large golden fruit in September–October. 'Champion' bears large, greenish-yellow, pear-shaped fruit. 'Vranja,' self-fertile, gives the largest production of fruit.

Decorative varieties are: 'Lusitanica,' with the largest leaves. 'Maliformis,' apple-shaped fruit. 'Marmorate,' leaves variegated with white and yellow. 'Pyramidalis,' with a pyramidal habit. 'Pyriformis,' with pear-shaped fruit.

111 EMBOTHRIUM COCCINEUM
Chilean Fire Bush

U.S. zone 9

Family Proteaceae.

Place of origin Chile and Argentina.

Description This semi- to almost evergreen tree or large shrub, 18–45 ft. (6–15m.) in cultivation, is particularly striking in May and June when it is covered in scarlet flowers. The leaves are alternate, lanceolate, oblong-eliptic to obovate, 2½–6 in. (6–15 m.) long, and a deep, quite lustrous green. The individual flowers are tubular, splitting to form 4 spoon-shaped, perianth segments, the head of each of which is concave bearing a stamen, crimson to orange-scarlet, often in great profusion.

Cultivation It prefers loose, open, non calcareous soil and a sheltered position. It should be planted in good loamy, peat-rich soil between April and May. It likes a mild climate but does not tolerate winds well. It looks particularly effective when planted among other trees and shrubs that will grow fairly tall or against a wall that will give shelter. If a compact shape is required, the incurving branches can be cut back by as much as half their length. Pruning should be done when the flowering season has finished, at the end of June–July. A dressing of fertilizer or manure is beneficial in early spring and about a spoonful of sulfate of potash per square yard (meter) can be given toward the end of summer.

Propagation By simple layering in spring or autumn. Seeds can be sown in April in a coldframe or cold greenhouse.

Winter protection In cold areas young plants should be protected by wrapping the branches in plastic sheeting but allowing air to circulate above and below. The base should also be mulched, all over the root area, with well-rotted leafmold or with peat.

Other species *E. coccineum* var. *longifolium* is also evergreen and has orange-scarlet flowers; it likes full sun or slight shade and needs to be protected from winds and frost.

112 ERIOBOTRYA JAPONICA
Loquat

Family Rosaceae.
Place of origin Japan and China.
Description This is the best known species of the genus *Eriobotrya* which comes from the Greek *erion*, "wool" and *botrys*, "a cluster of grapes" referring to the wooly flower clusters. The loquat is a small tree with a crowded, expansive, compact head, up to 20 ft. (6 m.) in height. It is grown for its glossy, evergreen foliage and its delicious fruits. Its large, obovate-elliptic, leathery leaves are nearly 10 in. (25 cm.) long and bright green, glossy on the upper surface, downy and reddish beneath. Its yellowish-white flowers are grouped in stiff terminal panicles. Its oblong fruit is about the size of a walnut with orange-yellow skin and pulp; it is juicy, edible and sweet and contains 3–7 large, shiny brown seeds.
Cultivation It is grown in mild climates where the early bloom is not likely to be harmed by frost. It likes loamy, well-manured soil and does not suffer in dry weather. It is easy to grow. Pruning should be done before the autumn flowering. It will not produce fruit in cooler, temperate climates, such as the British Isles.
Propagation By seed; the varieties by grafting.
Other species The most popular varieties are: 'Advance,' 'Early Red,' 'Premier,' 'Oliver' and 'Tanaka.'

---

113 EUONYMUS EUROPAEUS
Common Spindle Tree

Family Celastraceae.
Place of origin Europe.
Description A graceful deciduous shrub or small tree with an elegant crown, colorful ornamental fruits and brilliant autumn foliage. In the wild it grows freely in broadleaved woods, hedgerows and by streams, up to an altitude of about 2,560 ft. (800 m.). The branches, which can reach a height of 20 ft. (6 m.), are green when young, becoming brown with age. The leaves are opposite and lanceolate with a finely dentate margin. Its rather insignificant, greenish flowers are grouped in small cymes in clusters of 2–5. The fruits remain on the tree during the winter; these bright red, 4-lobed, poisonous capsules contain large seeds covered with orange pulp.
Cultivation It likes calcareous, clayey, damp, deep soil in the sun or in semishade. It also grows well in a tub. Give a spring dressing of fertilizer or manure and water regularly in dry weather. Any untidy branches can be cut out at the end of winter.
Propagation By seed or cuttings in September, by simple layering, or by detaching the stolons and bringing them on in a nursery bed. Transplanting can be done in autumn–winter.
Other species *E. alatus*, (Winged Euonymus), deciduous, very hardy; the leaves turn a beautiful soft rosy red in the autumn. New varieties that are very popular in the U.S. are called Burning Bush by nurserymen because they turn a brilliant deep red; this is supposed to be an improvement over the species but it is actually a very jarring color. *E. fortunei*, evergreen, frost-resistant.

114 FAGUS SYLVATICA
Beech

Family Fagaceae.

Place of origin Europe.

Description A large deciduous, ornamental tree whose dense foliage gives generous shade; if allowed to grow to its full height it will reach 100–150 ft. (30–45 m.). The color of the foliage, which ranges from light green in the spring and summer, shading to bronze in the autumn, gives it a particular elegance. The smooth gray bark that covers its great trunk is quite distinctive and the branches only spring from fairly low down if the tree is growing in an isolated position; usually, when surrounded by other trees, the branches emerge from high on the shaft. The leaves, positioned alternately on the long branches but in clusters on the short lateral branches, are oval with an undulate margin and are borne on short petioles. When young, the leaves are edged with white downy hairs and are a brilliant light green with lateral venation becoming smooth and shiny as the season advances. They are positioned in a mosaic-type pattern on each plane in order to obtain the maximum benefit from the light; even when dry they remain on the tree until expelled by the development of new buds.

The unisexual, petalless flowers appear at the same time as the leaves. The male flowers, each with 8–16 stamens, are borne in tassle-like clusters on slender, pendant stalks, the erect female flowers, in axillary clusters of 2, 3 or 4, are surrounded by 4 bracts and have 3 styles; they are quite inconspicuous.

The polished, reddish-brown fruits, known as beechnuts or beech mast, are triangular and enclosed in the 4 bracts of the female flower, which at this stage have become quite woody and covered with rigid but not prickly bristles. This capsule opens up when ripe. At one time the beech mast, which is edible, was used to provide fodder for herds of swine, which were grazed in woodlands. Fruiting does not occur every year or on old trees.

The natural habitat of the beech is in broadleaved woods from the hilly to the montane regions where the species may grow by itself to form beech woods or with other trees such as oak or fir and spruce trees.

Cultivation Beech trees will grow in any type of ground providing that it is well-drained and acid and not too hard or damp. Although they are sun-loving, they also thrive in shady positions. The young plants should be transplanted with great care and kept well-watered until the roots are thoroughly established. Beech can be used for hedging, windbreaks or screens, the young plants being spaced 20 ins. (50 cm.) from each other. Pruning should be done at the end of the summer.

Propagation By seed in the spring, by division of the root suckers.

Other taxa *F. sylvatica* 'Purpurea Tricolor,' with purplish foliage edged with rose and pinkish white. *F. sylvatica* 'Asplenifolia' (Fern-leaved Beech), with deeply serrate green leaves. *F. sylvatica* 'Pendula,' with pendulous branches. *F. sylvatica* forma *quercoides*, with rough, cracked bark. *F. sylvatica* forma *tortuosa*, with twisted branches. *F. grandifolia*, from North America, with large, narrow leaves and a suckering habit. *F. orientalis* (*F. sylvatica* var. *macrophylla*) with large green leaves.

115 FRAXINUS ORNUS
Manna Ash

U.S. zone 5

Family Oleaceae.
Place of origin Europe.
Description A small deciduous tree that attains a height of 50–66 ft. (16–20 m.), it has a full rounded, elegant head with ascendant branches. Its leaves consist of 5–9 elliptic, petiolate leaflets, each 1⅛–2¾ in. (28–70 mm.) long, with an acuminate tip. "Manna" is obtained from cuts in the stems; it is a rubbery, sweet, descending sap at one time used pharmaceutically as a sugar. The pinkish-white, scented flowers, with their 4-petaled corollas, are grouped in closely-packed panicles. The fruits consist of long samaras that are winged at the tip.

A feature that distinguishes the manna ash from other ashes is its late flowering, which may come when the leaves appear or later. The tree's natural habitat is woodland.
Cultivation A good pioneer species because it improves soil fertility; it is suitable for reforestation in poor and calcareous ground and in fire-damaged woods. The manna ash is an ornamental tree, often grown in parks and gardens for its foliage, its perfumed flowers and for its "manna." It is very cold-resistant, grows well even in poor soil and easily throws up new suckers.
Propagation By seed, by simple layering, by root suckers.
Other species *F. americana* (White Ash), its leaflets have whitish undersides. *F. excelsior*, (European or Common Ash), a deciduous tree with a broad crown. *F. oxycarpa* (*F. oxyphylla*), a small deciduous tree with a narrowly domed crown. The samaras are not pointed.

---

116 HAMAMELIS MOLLIS
Chinese Witch Hazel

U.S. zone 6

Family Hamamelidaceae.
Place of origin China.
Description A bushy deciduous, slow-growing shrub or tree up to 30 ft. (9 m.) high. It has decorative foliage that changes color in the autumn and flowers during the winter on bare branches. Its obovate leaves are about 4 in. (10 cm.) long, glossy on the upper surface and densely downy beneath, with a dentate margin; green during the spring and summer, turning red and then yellow in autumn. The delicately scented flowers, about ¾ in. (2 cm.) across, are very attractive with 4 yellow petals and a deep red calyx. The fruit, which is rather like a hazelnut, takes a year to ripen and remains on the plant during the following year's flowering.
Cultivation The witch hazel is hardy and very cold-resistant. It needs loamy, well-drained soil and a sunny position facing north; in a mild climate it prefers semishade; it should be sheltered from the wind. It requires plenty of water, especially during dry weather. Pruning is not necessary. Witch hazel can also be grown in a large pot.
Propagation Preferably by grafting or by seed in the autumn, by air layering, by simple layering.
Other species *H.* 'Pallida,' with particularly lovely pale yellow flowers. *H. invernalis*, originating from North America, has scented yellow flowers. *H. japonica*, deciduous, with yellow flowers and red-yellow leaves in the autumn. *H. virginiana*, a hardier plant with yellow flowers when the leaves fall.

117 HIBISCUS ROSA-SINENSIS
Chinese Hibiscus

Family Malvaceae.

Place of origin Tropical Asia.

Description A shrub from subtropical climates where it attains a height of 9 ft. (3 m.); in cultivation it is only half as tall. It has an open, expansive habit and is widely distributed throughout the warm-hot regions where its ornamental and colorful presence can be seen in nearly every garden from the West Indies to the Mediterranean. Its glossy green leaves, which in hotter areas are evergreen, are slightly ovate to ovate-lanceolate and sometimes pointed toward the base. Its bright red, solitary flowers are 3⅛–4 in. (8–10 cm.) in diameter, their most attractive feature being their prominent stamens and pistil. There are also cultivars with yellow, apricot or pink, single or double flowers.

Cultivation In order to live in the open ground throughout the year, the hibiscus requires favorable climatic conditions. In warm-hot climates it can easily be grown outdoors in a sunny position, in rich, loamy soil that should always be kept moist. It can be pruned in the autumn after it has flowered.

Winter protection This is essential in cooler, temperate climates, where the hibiscus will not survive the winter outdoors. In such conditions it can be grown in a large pot (even though it needs to be pruned more severely than when growing in the open), which can be brought indoors during the cold season as soon as the temperature falls below 46–50°F (8–10°C).

Propagation By seed, by softwood cuttings rooted in a mixture of sand and peat between spring and summer.

Other species *H. schizopetalus*, from tropical Africa, with orange-red flowers. *H. trionum*, an annual with yellow or white flowers with purple centers.

Family   Leguminosae.

Place of origin   Southern Europe.

Description   This is a deciduous tree up to 30 ft. (10 m.) high, with erect, green branches. Its trifoliate leaves are downy when young and paler on the underside, borne on long stalks. The numerous yellow flowers, falling in pendulous, showy racemes 8–12 in. (20–30 cm.) long are followed by pods containing poisonous seeds.

The laburnum is cultivated for its decorative, sweetly scented flowers and glossy leaves as well as for the beneficial effect it has on poor ground by returning nitrogen to the soil. It is also used to prevent soil erosion in particularly vulnerable areas such as on hillsides. The pods are believed to be particularly poisonous when fresh.

It is sometimes referred to as "false ebony" because it seems that, in antiquity, its hard, pliable, elastic wood was used to make bows. Today it is used to make hoops for barrels and, because it is finely veined and polishes well, it is a favorite material for chairs and wind instruments. Because it is knot-resistant, it is also used in small garden furnishings.

Cultivation   It requires deep, moist, calcareous soil and to be sited in the sun in cold climates, and in semishade in warmer areas. The laburnum is pruned, not so much to keep the plant in shape as to remove dead or damaged branches.

Propagation   By seed, by grafting, by cuttings.

Other taxa   *L. alpinum*, rather smaller, with pendulous racemes of scented flowers and glossy leaves. *L. anagyroides* 'Aureum,' with golden leaves. *L. × watereri* 'Vossii,' golden racemes, up to 2 ft. (62 cm.) long.

LAGERSTROEMIA INDICA
Crape Myrtle U.S. zone 7

Family Lythraceae.
Place of origin China and Korea.
Description Linnaeus, the father of modern botany, dedicated this genus to his friend Magnus von Lagerström (1696–1759) the Swedish manager of the East India Company. *L. indica* was introduced into Europe in 1759 marking the beginning of its great popularity. It was to become for warm regions what the lilac and viburnum are to northern areas – a plant to be seen in nearly every garden and patio.

The crape myrtle is a small deciduous tree with a very sturdy trunk attaining a height of 23 ft. (7 m.). The branches are twisted and smooth. Its small, elliptic leaves have a pointed tip; they are 1–2 in. (2.5–5 cm.) long, turning to red and yellow in the autumn. The flowers are gathered in terminal panicles up to 8 in. (20 cm.) long; they are pink, white or violet and have six undulate petals.

The crape myrtle is grown mainly in warm regions either as a single plant or to line streets. Its summer bloom is very decorative and it is particularly welcome at a time of the year when there are not many flowering perennials.

Cultivation It requires clayey, damp soil, rich in manure and humus. It is hardy and prefers a sunny position. It tolerates an urban atmosphere. The branches should be pruned in February to shorten the previous year's growth. The plant can also be grown in a container in a cool greenhouse.

Winter protection In very cold areas, where it should be grown in a container, it can be put under cover.

Propagation By seed in the spring, by cuttings in the summer.

Other species *L. speciosa*, with flowers ranging from pink to violet.

120 LAURUS NOBILIS
Bay Tree, Bay Laurel

Family Lauraceae.

Place of origin The Mediterranean region.

Description An evergreen tree, pyramidal in shape, and typical of the Mediterranean region, where it grows wild in open woodland, in dry positions, on slopes and along the coast. It reaches a maximum height of about 40–60 ft. (13–20 m.). The bay tree is cultivated for its scented flowers, aromatic fruits and glossy leaves, which can be used for culinary and medicinal purposes. It has a shrubby habit with a dense crown and abundant branches right down to the base. Its leathery, alternate leaves are about 4 in. (10 cm.) across, lanceolate and elliptic with an undulate margin; they are glossy, green and aromatic. The unisexual, aromatic, yellow flowers are grouped in loose axillary clusters, each with its 4 petals supported by bracts. The male flowers have 8–12 stamens and the females have a pistil and 4 sterile stamens. The fruits are borne on the female plants; they are black, oval, shiny drupes, rather like olives, containing a large, hard seed and an oil that keeps mosquitoes away.

In antiquity the bay was regarded as a symbol of achievement and glory for poets, winners of athletic events and conquerors, a crown of its leaves being placed on their heads in celebration.

Cultivation A hardy plant, typical of maritime and lakeside areas in mild climates, where it can withstand the cold. It can be pruned, even to the extent of making a hedge. It is also used in warmer regions to line streets or to provide shade and can be grown in a pot. It grows in any type of soil provided that it is fertile and manured. Bay trees need to be in the sun and sheltered from the wind; they require regular watering in dry summer weather. To ensure fruiting, there should always be male and female plants. To create a hedge, the young plants are spaced at intervals of 12 in. (30 cm.).

Winter protection In places where severe cold weather is likely to persist, the plants should be mulched around the roots.

Propagation By seed, by cuttings in the autumn, by division of the basal suckers, by air layering.

Other species *L. nobilis* forma *angustifolia* has very narrow leaves. *L. nobilis* forma *crispa* has wavy leaf margins. *L. azorica* (*L. canariensis*), originating from the Canary Islands and the Azores, has much larger leaves and downy twigs.

MAGNOLIA GRANDIFLORA
Southern Magnolia   **U.S. zone 7**

Family Magnoliaceae.

Place of origin North America.

Description A large evergreen tree, which can attain a height of about 90 ft. (28 m.), but is often much less in gardens. Its ornamental qualities lie in its large, glossy leaves and large, waxy, perfumed flowers. The straight trunk is branched from the base and its spreading, pyramid-shaped crown reaches a width of up to 26 ft. (8 m.). Its smooth, gray bark has medicinal properties and the branches, when young, are downy and reddish in color. Its large, alternate, deep green, glossy leaves are brown on the underside; they are entire, elliptic and leathery with a short, hairy petiole. Its large, solitary, yellowish-white flowers, which smell of lemons, stand out well in contrast to the dark leaves. Flowering takes place throughout the summer and autumn. Its brown fruits, supported on stalks, are erect and rather similar to pine cones; they are about 4 in. (10 cm.) long with red seeds that emerge on ripening. It is very long-lived and slow-growing. The generic name is dedicated to the French botanist Pierre Magnol (1638–1715).

Cultivation The southern magnolia grows best in a mild climate but will survive in cold areas against a wall in a sheltered position. It prefers not to be exposed to the full sun and likes a well-drained, slightly acid soil, provided that it is not calcareous or clayey, enriched with peat or well-rotted garden compost. It does not like the frost, and snow can damage its branches. It needs constant moisture. Pruning will not harm it and a light trim to keep the plant in shape may be necessary but it is better to allow the plant to expand freely.

Winter protection Young plants should be protected with plastic sheeting or covered frames.

Propagation By seed in the autumn, by cuttings, by air layering, by simple layering, by grafting.

Other taxa *M. grandiflora* 'Gallissonniere,' one of the hardiest cultivars; its leaves have a reddish tinge on the lower surface and white flowers with 12 petals. *M. grandiflora* 'Exmouth' ('Lanceolata,' 'Exoniensis'), rather fastigiate in habit, its leaves are red underneath. *M. grandiflora* 'Goliath' has white flowers up to 1 ft. (30 cm.) wide. *M. delavayi*, originally from China, this tree attains a height of about 33 ft. (10 cm.) and does not like frost; it bears scented white flowers. *M. virginiana* (*M. glauca*, Sweet Bay), with semipersistent leaves, its white flowers have 7–12 petals, flowering June–September.

122 MAGNOLIA LILIIFLORA

Family Magnoliaceae.
Place of origin China.
Description A deciduous shrub or very small tree growing to only 13 ft. (4 m.). Its dark green leaves are about 8 in. (20 cm.) long with a pointed tip. Its large, white flowers, stained red on the outside, have six big petals that never open fully and remain erect. The flowering period lasts from April–June and there is sometimes a secondary flowering at the end of the summer.
Cultivation It flourishes in areas with a mild climate. It likes to be sited in full sun or semishade, sheltered from the frost, in loamy, well-manured, siliceous, moist ground. It withstands the cold quite well.
Winter protection Young plants should be protected.
Propagation By seed, by air layering, by simple layering, by grafting.
Other species These are all deciduous: *M. acuminata* (Cucumber Tree), from North America, has greenish-yellow, unscented, rather inconspicuous flowers with 6–8 petals; its cucumber-like fruits turn red on ripening. *M. fraseri*, with large, scented flowers. *M. macrophylla*, with leaves up to about 32 in. (80 cm.) long, very large scented flowers and pink fruits. *M. tripetala* (Umbrella Tree), a tree to about 50 ft. (15 m.) high, with large, beautiful leaves. *M. kobus*, from Japan, has small, starry flowers and decorative, pink, stemmed fruits with red seeds. *M. hypoleuca*, with long, red fruits. *M. stellata* (Star Magnolia), from Japan, has solitary white flowers with 10–18 open petals; it blooms very early in the spring. *M. denudata*, originating from China, has numerous white, scented flowers in the spring.

---

123 MAGNOLIA × SOULANGIANA

Family Magnoliaceae.
Place of origin Cultivated.
Description A small deciduous tree with a spreading, elegant crown and numerous branches. It attains a height of about 17 ft. (5 m.) and sometimes has a shrubby habit. It is the most popular species in general cultivation and was achieved by crossing *M. denudata* and *M. liliiflora*. The cup-shaped flowers up to 10 in. (25 cm.) across are white or pink to purple, depending on the cultivar. They appear when the plant is only a few years old. As the flowering ends the leaves begin to break; these are obovate, coarse and about 4 in. (10 cm.) long. The species is named for E. Soulange-Bodin who raised the hybrid in 1820. This magnolia can be grown by itself or with other species.
Cultivation It requires little space but needs deep, well-manured, acid, moist soil. Shade it from the sun in fairly hot areas and shelter it from the wind. It thrives in a mild climate although it withstands the cold well.
Winter protection Young plants should be protected.
Propagation By cuttings, by simple layering, by air layering. Cultivation from seed is a very slow process.
Other taxa *M. × soulangiana* 'Alba,' with white flowers. *M. × soulangiana* 'Alexandrina,' with red flowers. *M. × soulangiana* 'Rustica rubra,' with white flowers stained red outside.

124 MALUS FLORIBUNDA
Japanese Flowering Crab

U.S. zone 5

Family Rosaceae.
Place of origin Japan. Introduced into Europe about 1862.
Description A tree up to 30 ft. (9 m.) with arching branches and ovate, dentate, green leaves. Its magnificent crimson flower buds become red as they mature, turning pink on opening. Its small, round, yellow fruits are ¾ in. (2 cm.) in diameter. It looks particularly lovely when grown by itself on a well-tended lawn; it looks equally pretty in a shrubbery border.
Cultivation The Japanese crab can be sited in full sun or semishade. It is quite tolerant as to soil type but gives better results if this is enriched with well-rotted manure or other good humus. It is planted during mild weather when the ground is not too wet. The hole should be large enough to contain the spread-out roots. The soil should be enriched with bonemeal. Thereafter a dressing of general fertilizer or well-rotted manure should be applied every spring.
Propagation By grafting in July or August. It is possible to raise from seed but this is a tedious process.
Other species *M. hupehensis*, a vigorous species with a rigid habit, it has an abundance of scented white flowers that are pink when in bud. *M. × purpurea* has dark red buds which become paler on flowering, leaves purplish red.

---

125 MESPILUS GERMANICA
Medlar

U.S. zone 6

Family Rosaceae.
Place of origin Asia Minor and Europe.
Description A small deciduous tree, sometimes having a shrubby habit, attaining a height of 20 ft. (6 m.), with short, often spiny branches; (the cultivated varieties are not always spiny). It has an untidy, spreading crown and the young branches are hairy. Its sessile leaves are fasciculate, lanceolate and pointed; they are bright green and velvety with a padded appearance on the upper surface, hairy and grayish beneath. The flowers, which grow singly, have 5 separate white petals with red stamens and are surrounded by the leaves on short branches. The fruit is a small, round, light brown apple, flattened at the extremities, surmounted by the remains of the 5 sepals and containing 5 nuts. It has medicinal qualities and is edible, becoming sweet and flavorful only when picked before ripening and left to become overripe.
  The medlar tree grows wild in broadleaved woodlands, hedgerows and on stony slopes up to an altitude of about 3,280 ft. (1,000 m.). It is rarely cultivated nowadays.
Cultivation The medlar tree needs fairly dry, deep, well-drained, manured, clayey or stony soil and a sunny or shaded position; warmth is essential. It is slow-growing, undemanding and adapts to most climates. It withstands cold and generally bad weather.
Propagation By air layering, by grafting. Raising medlar trees from seed is a very slow process.
Other taxa Several cultivars have large or early fruit.

126 PRUNUS AVIUM
Mazzard, Gean

Family Rosaceae.
Place of origin Europe.
Description A tree 30–60 ft. (10–20 m.) tall, having a straight trunk 20–28 in. (50–70 cm.) in diameter with glossy bark. The oval, acuminate leaves are a shiny, bronzy-brown turning to pale green. Its white flowers are 1 in. (2.5 cm.) in diameter. The fruit is a reddish-black, pendulous, round drupe, ¾ in. (2 cm.) in diameter with a sweet taste. There are several cultivars.
Cultivation It requires deep, well-drained, not too calcareous soil and moisture. In its wild state it grows well in mountains and, when cultivated, requires a temperate or temperate-cold climate. A regular dressing of a balanced fertilizer or manure is beneficial and the ground around the roots should be cultivated every winter. In the spring and summer the surrounding area should be kept free of weeds. Pruning should be limited to keeping the tree in a roughly pyramidal shape. In very porous or gravelly soil the tree should be kept watered from late May, if the weather is hot and dry, and during the summer if the ground is likely to dry out.
Propagation By seed.

127 PRUNUS PERSICA
Peach

Family Rosaceae.
Place of origin At one time the peach was believed to have originated from Persia but, in 1855, the Swiss botanist Alphonse De Candolle asserted that its provenance was China, where it grows wild.
Description It grows to 10–27 ft. (3–8 m.), and has a rather twisted trunk and many branches. Its graceful lanceolate leaves are green on the upper surface and grayish beneath, with a serrate margin. The flowers grow singly in the leaf axils; they are borne on the previous year's growth and emerge before the leaves appear; they are pale pink and 1–1½ in. (2.5–4 cm.) in diameter. The fruits are round, fleshy, velvety drupes, 2–3⅛ in. (5–8 cm.) across but larger in the cultivars. There are numerous flowering cultivars with single or double flowers of various shades.
Cultivation The peach requires loose, deep, porous soil, even if stony. A heavy clay or cold, damp soil with nonporous subsoil will strangle the tree and cause chlorosis (yellowing of the leaves) ultimately resulting in its death. In calcareous soil the peach may suffer from chlorosis if it has not been grafted on to almond stock. It prefers a mild climate but does not like too much warmth because, if it does not have a certain number of hours of cold, where the temperature drops below 45°F (7°C), it does not have a long enough resting period and the buds are damaged.
Propagation By seed, by grafting.

128 PRUNUS SERRULATA

Family Rosaceae.
Place of origin China.
Description A tree to 25 ft. (7 m.) high with dark brown, smooth bark. Its deep green leaves are ovate to ovate-acuminate and acute with a serrate margin. The white flowers are double or semidouble, 1–1½ in. (2.5–4 cm.) in diameter, grouped in clusters of 2–5, each being borne on a short or long stalk. The fruit is small, black and round. This species is a great favorite and is to be seen in its typical form as well as in its many cultivars, the flowers of which may be white or pink.
Cultivation It likes a mild, temperate climate and grows easily in a light, sunny position. It grows in any ordinary, well-drained soil and is suitable for growing in fairly shallow soil, even with a calcareous subsoil.
Propagation By hardwood cuttings.
Other species *P. × yedoensis*, with very abundant white or pink flowers.

---

129 PRUNUS SUBHIRTELLA
Winter Flowering Cherry

Family Rosaceae.
Place of origin Japan.
Description An exceptionally ornamental tree up to 30 ft. (9 m.) tall, described by some as the most beautiful Japanese flowering cherry. The branches are erect and the leaves fairly narrow and rather short. The flowers vary from white to pink with a reddish calyx. It comes into bloom before the leaves appear and a distinctive feature is its tendency also to produce flowers in the autumn, although not every year. There are many cultivars such as var. *pendula* with its procumbent branches and 'Autumnalis,' a shrubby form with semidouble, pink flowers and slender, spreading branches. The former, called the Weeping Higan Cherry, is especially popular in the U.S.
Cultivation A hardy tree that likes an open, sunny position. It adapts easily to any type of soil provided this is not soggy. It does not need feeding.
Propagation By hardwood cuttings.
Other species *P. glandulosa* 'Rosea Plena,' with double, pink flowers. *P. humilis*, a bush 4–5 ft. (1–1½ m.) with pale pink flowers, and red fruits.

130 PUNICA GRANATUM
Pomegranate

Family Punicaceae.

Place of origin Iran and Afghanistan.

Description A small, sun-loving tree, widespread in the wild wherever there is a Mediterranean climate, from Asia Minor to the south of France. It is mainly grown in country gardens for its ornamental flowers and fruit and also because of the ancient traditions with which it is associated. Religious significance has been attributed to the pomegranate fruit since antiquity, and to the Phoenicians it was a symbol of fertility. The pomegranate, like the fig and the grapevine, was one of the first conquests to have been made by neolithic farmers in western Asia. The Phoenicians in Carthage were the first people in North Africa to grow the pomegranate and the Romans believed it to have originated there. Cato called this fruit *malum punicum*, meaning "Carthaginian apple," while L. M. Columella defined it as *malum granatum*, "the apple with grain-like seeds." (It is interesting to note that the precious stone known as a garnet derives from the Latin word for the pomegranate.)

It is a deciduous, well-branched tree 15 ft. (5 m.) high. In late spring it puts out small, shiny, oval leaves and by June is covered with bright red flowers, each with a long fleshy calyx. By October the pomegranate fruits are ripe; they have a tough, leathery skin to protect the soft center, which is divided internally into about 12 compartments in which are enclosed the woody seeds, each surrounded by a layer of very juicy pulp.

Cultivation The pomegranate needs to be in a sunny position, against the wall of a house or wherever it will not be exposed to the wind or frost. Hardier and more resistant than the citruses, it grows anywhere except in mountainous areas, and will do well in any fertile and well-drained soil. Since the branches tend to grow rather untidily, they should be thinned in the spring to let in the light and air so the tree will produce flowers and fruit. Young plants require regular watering in the spring. The fruits tend to split if left to ripen on the tree; they should therefore be picked while still unripe and left to continue the process indoors.

Propagation Cuttings about 10–12 in. (25–30 cm.) long can be taken between February and March and rooted in sand in a warm propagating frame.

Other species *P. granatum* var. *nana*, (Dwarf Pomegranate), grows to about 2 ft. (⅓ m.) and has smaller leaves, flowers and fruit.

131 SALIX CAPREA
Goat Willow, Great Sallow

U.S. zone 5

Family Salicaceae.
Place of origin Europe and northwest Asia.
Description A small deciduous tree that grows to a height of 25 ft. (7½ m.). Its branches are short and rough, but downy when young. Its alternate leaves are oval or rounded with an entire margin and 1⅛–4 in. (3–10 cm.) across. The flowers make their appearance before the leaves in very striking spikes; the male flowers are yellow catkins about 1¼ in. (3 cm.) long, and the female flowers are green, about 4 in. (10 cm.) long, covered with silvery down and have black bracts. The fruits expand into feathery seeds. Goat willow grows wild on the edge of woods, in hedgerows and abandoned quarries.
Cultivation The goat willow likes moist, well-manured ground, even if it is clayey, and a sunny or semishaded position. It is very hardy and can withstand the cold well. It is a decorative plant, useful for planting in wet ground where little else will grow.
Propagation By cuttings in the autumn and spring.
Other species *S. alba* 'Britzensis,' in which the first-year stems turn bright red in winter. *S. babylonica* (Weeping Willow). *S. daphnoides* (Violet Willow), with reddish branches. *S. matsudana* 'Tortuosa,' with twisted branches. *S. viminalis* (Common Osier), with long, slender flexible branches. *S. × boydii*, with silvery leaves, is a dwarf shrub and ideal for rock gardens. *S.* 'Chrysocoma' (Golden Weeping Willow), a large weeping willow.

132 ZIZIPHUS JUJUBA
(syn. *Z. sativa*)
Jujube

U.S. zone 7

Family Rhamnaceae.
Place of origin Asia.
Description A small deciduous tree attaining a height of up to 30 ft. (9 m.). The glossy foliage and elegant crown are very decorative and its fruits are sweet and edible as well as having medicinal properties. The bark is grooved and the branches spiny. The twigs that have borne fruit fall with the leaves. Its alternate, glossy green leaves are ovate with pointed tip and a finely dentate margin. The small, starry flowers are yellowish. The jujube has a large drupe containing a nut, rather like an olive, with a shiny brown skin and an indented apex; it is sweet and of great medicinal value.
Cultivation It is a long-lived, slow-growing plant. It likes open, fertile well-manured soil and needs to be watered constantly in dry weather. It can withstand the cold in a mild climate but is not hardy in temperate regions. The jujube tree likes to be in a sunny position, sheltered from the wind.
Propagation By division of the basal suckers in the winter.
Other species *Z. lotus*, with undulate, spiny branches and small, round, edible fruits. *Z. spina-christi*, with spiny branches and edible fruits, useful as a shade tree.

133 ACTINIDIA DELICIOSA
(syn. *A. chinensis*)
Kiwi, Kiwi Fruit, Chinese Gooseberry **U.S. zone 7**

Family Actinidiaceae.

Place of origin China.

Description A woody, climbing, deciduous plant, grown for its green-fleshed fruit as well as for its decorative foliage. The alternate, ovate, dark green leaves are downy and from 6–8 in. (15–20 cm.) long. Its slightly scented flowers are white turning to brown, up to 2 in. (5 cm.) across. The greenish-brown fruits are large, oval-rounded, hairy berries about 2 in. (5 cm.) long; they have a pleasant scent and are edible and vitamin-rich. *A. deliciosa* is a dioecious plant and only the female plants bear fruit. It is widely cultivated in New Zealand and Southern California.

Cultivation It is hardy but requires mild climatic conditions without wide differences in temperature. It requires special care, rather like that given to grapevines. The soil should be rich in humus, non calcareous, moist and well-drained. The plant needs to be sited in a warm, sunny position or in semishade, sheltered from the wind and from excessive heat from the sun. As it may grow as tall as 26 ft. (8 m.) under ideal conditions, it needs some kind of support and is well-suited to being trained up arches, pergolas and columns. Plants grown on wire mainly for their fruit are planted at intervals of at least 13 ft. (4 m.). As these are dioecious plants, there should always be several in fairly close proximity, with a ratio of one male to 1–5 females; alternatively, a branch from a male plant can be grafted on to a female plant.

Pruning is important and must be done accurately and annually. While still young, the plant needs only to be kept in shape, but, once it has fruited the shoots that have borne fruit on the female plants and the branches that have flowered on the male plants should be cut back in late winter in order to obtain a really good crop. *Actinidia* does not react well to springtime frosts or dryness and needs to be kept regularly watered in the spring and summer when the weather is dry.

Winter protection In colder areas the woody branches of young trees should be protected with plastic sheeting and the roots mulched.

Propagation By seed under glass, by air layering, by simple layering, by hardwood cuttings in the winter, by semihardwood cuttings in the autumn and by softwood cuttings in the summer. Transplanting can be done in the autumn.

Other species They all originate from East Asia. *A. arguta*, a climbing, dioecious plant that may grow to a height of over 33 ft. (10 m.) is intolerant of spring frosts; it has scented white flowers, red leaf branches and edible, sweet, vitamin-rich fruits. *A. coriacea*, a climber with small, deep pink, scented flowers and small, oval, brown fruits; it does not withstand the cold well. *A. kolomikta*, a very decorative, hardy climber able to withstand frost; its branches need to be pruned and shaped; the leaves are variegated green, white and red; it is a dioecious plant with bluish-black, sweet, edible fruits that are richer in vitamins than *A. deliciosa*; it is sometimes known as "the cats' plant" because of its attractiveness to cats. *A. polygama*, a silvery vine, is particularly attractive to cats; its leaves are silvery, variegated with yellow; it has scented white flowers and yellow fruit, about 1½ in. (4 cm.) long, which is edible but not very tasty.

134 BIGNONIA CAPREOLATA

(syn. *Doxantha capreolata*)
Cross Vine

U.S. zone 6

Family Bignoniaceae.

Place or origin Southeastern United States.

Description This is a vigorous, evergreen, climber; it is hardy in a mild climate but its leaves are inclined to fall when the climate does not suit it. It grows to about 40 ft. (12 m.) in the wild, using its axillary paw-shaped tendrils as suction cups. Its lanceolate, rigid, shiny green leaves are 2–6 in. (5–15 cm.) long and positioned in opposite pairs with the branched tendrils. Its distinctively scented flowers are borne in clusters and are 2 in. (5 cm.) long with a tubular calyx opening out into 5 short, backward-curving lobes. Their color, which is paler inside the calyx, ranges from red to orange, according to the climate. A latitudinal cross section of the stem reveals an unusual type of cross, hence its common name. The generic name, *Bignonia*, is dedicated to the Abbé Bignon and the synonym, *Doxantha*, means "glory of the flowers," referring to the lovely bright inflorescence.

Cultivation It likes light, air, space and plenty of water in the summer, but watering should be reduced when the plant is in flower and discontinued during the winter. It has no particular soil preference and grows well in a container. All superfluous branches should be cut out; those remaining can be shortened to encourage especially fine flowers.

Winter protection Protection is necessary if cold weather persists.

Propagation By seed, by simple layering, by semihardwood cuttings.

---

135 BOUGAINVILLEA GLABRA

U.S. zone 10

Family Nyctaginaceae.

Place of origin Brazil.

Description A flowering climber, giving a brilliant purplish display, it is ideal for covering walls, pergolas and arches. Its woody main stem grows up to about 50 ft. (15 m.) long and its curved spines, in the leaf axils, enable it to cling to whatever support is available. The alternate, shiny green leaves are ovate and smooth. The tubular, yellow flowers, in groups of 3, are quite insignificant on their own, but each one is supported by 3 very decorative purple bracts gathered at the tip of the branches.

Cultivation *Bougainvillea* can also be grown as a bush or in a tub. It thrives in a sunny place if given regular watering while in bloom. It grows in any kind of soil except clay. A popular plant in warm-hot regions, it flowers continuously from the spring to the autumn. In mild climates it should be in a sunny position, sheltered against a wall and protected from the wind. It is important to prune at the end of the winter by shortening the lateral branches to encourage new flowering shoots; for the same reason, the flowering sprays should be removed when they are over to encourage a secondary bloom in October.

Winter protection The roots should be mulched or a framework of plastic sheeting put over the plant in areas with a mild climate. Tubs must be put under cover.

Propagation By cuttings in July, by air layering, by simple layering.

Other species *B.* × *buttiana*, with pink bracts. *B. peruviana*, with pink bracts. *B. spectabilis*, with smaller bracts, less hardy.

136 CAMPSIS RADICANS
(syn. *Bignonia radicans, Tecoma radicans*)
Trumpet Vine   U.S. zone 5

Family Bignoniaceae.
Place of origin North America.
Description A vigorous deciduous climber up to 40 ft. (12 m.), it will cover old walls or trellises with ease. It is inclined to harbor ants. Its imparipinnate leaves, with 7–11 leaflets, are positioned opposite each other on the stems, which have numerous aerial roots. Its bell-like flowers are scarlet tinged with yellow inside the throat; they are 2¾–3⅛ in. (7–8 cm.) long, gathered into showy pendulous clusters on the current year's branches. The filaments of the stamens are curved.
Cultivation The trumpet vine prefers a sunny position. It needs deep, fertile, permeable soil that is humus-rich. It should be given a dressing of balanced fertilizer or manure in the latter part of the winter and regular watering in dry weather. Shelter it from the wind, because, as a result of its prolific growth, it may be blown down. The plant can be pruned to remove old and inactive branches as well as any new branches that may be causing overcrowding. This can be done when flowering has ended; at that time the whole plant can be lightly trimmed to control the size or, if necessary, drastically pruned if frost has caused a lot of damage. Basal suckers should be removed.
Winter protection If the weather is really harsh and persistent, the plant should be sheltered in a greenhouse.
Propagation By woody or root cuttings, by simple layering, by air layering.
Other species *C. grandiflora*, a less hardy climber, from China. *C.* × *tagliabuana*, with salmon-orange flowers.

---

137 CLEMATIS MONTANA
U.S. zone 6

Family Ranunculaceae.
Place of origin China and the Himalayas.
Description *C. montana* grows rapidly, to a maximum height of 40 ft. (12 m.) and therefore needs some kind of support which the small leaf stalks can grasp. The leaves are trifoliate and the flowers pink or white with 4 petaliform sepals, 1⅛–3⅛ in. (3–8 cm.) across.
Cultivation Since *C. montana* flowers on the previous year's wood, the plant should be lightly pruned just after it has finished flowering to keep it tidy. If, however, any of the aerial branches have been damaged by cold weather, these should be pruned quite hard in the spring. The roots must be kept in shade. It is ideal for covering walls or pergolas and is particularly effective when growing against a large tree. It likes moist, well-drained soil and to be mulched with humus in the spring; this serves to feed the roots and keep them cool and moist. It can be grown in a container.
Propagation By seed in the latter part of the winter, by air layering, by cuttings. It can be transplanted in spring or autumn after it has been cut back to about 12 in. (30 cm.) from the ground. It should be sunk to a depth of about 4 in. (10 cm.) below the surface to strengthen it and to protect it from the cold.
Other species *C. montana* 'Grandiflora,' with large, pinkish-white flowers. *C. montana* var. *rubens*, with purple-tinted young foliage and pinkish-mauve flowers. *C. montana* 'Tetrarose,' with deep rosy-red flowers. *C. montana* var. *wilsonii*, with large pure white flowers in July–August.

Family Araliaceae.

Place of origin Europe and western Asia.

Description An evergreen climber that clings to tree trunks, house walls and supports of almost any kind. In classical culture ivy was used for its medicinal properties.

Its woody stems climb to about 60 ft. (20 m.) and it clings on by means of adhesive roots that do not parasitize the host tree; it branches freely, always growing away from the light as it creeps or climbs by means of negative phototropism. Its small, stemmed leaves are alternate, varying in size from 1½–4¾ in. (4–12 cm.) across. They are smooth, shiny and persistent, light green when young and darkening with age. The shapes also vary through elliptic, cordate and triangular, with 3–5 lobes.

The flower-bearing terminal branches grow toward the light. They bear entire ovate or elliptic leaves, quite different from those on the sterile branches. The tiny greenish-yellow flowers appear in late summer in terminal umbels; they are very attractive to bees and other insects. Each little flower consists of 5 petals and 5 stamens. Wind-pollination (anemophily) and self-pollination facilitate fruiting and the opaque, yellowish berries, which turn blue-black as they ripen in the spring, are probably poisonous. The common or English ivy is very long-lived and is very common in warm and temperate regions.

Cultivation Ivy likes rich, humid, clayey ground. It withstands the cold well but does not grow above an altitude of about 4,000 ft. (1,200 m.). It likes shade or semishade to full sun. It is generally grown as groundcover or to cover walls, pergolas, tree trunks or arches but it is also grown in tubs. When transplanting, the plant should be lightly tied to the support until its adventitious roots have had time to take hold. It requires watering if the soil is dry. Ivy can be trimmed almost any time, but usually in the spring.

Propagation By cutting in the summer or autumn.

Other taxa *H. helix* 'Acerifolia,' the leaves of which have deep, sinuous lobes. *H. helix* 'Digitata,' the leaves of which have equal, palmate lobes. *H. helix* 'Pedata,' leaves with long, narrow lobes. *H. helix* 'Hibernica' (Irish Ivy), with very large leaves. *H. helix* 'Glacier,' with silvery-gray leaves. *H. helix* 'Goldheart,' with small leaves, the centers of which have yellow markings. *H. canariensis* with large, heart-shaped leaves and red stalks. *H. canariensis* 'Gloire de Marengo,' a very decorative climber with silvery-gray, variegated leaves. *H. colchica*, a robust plant with leaves about 8 in. (20 cm.) long.

139 JASMINUM NUDIFLORUM
Winter Jasmine

Family Oleaceae.
Place of origin China.
Description A deciduous shrub with a rambling habit; it is useful for covering tree trunks, walls and hedges and attains a length of about 10 ft. (3 m.). The green leaves, arranged in opposite pairs on the quadrangular branches, are trifoliate. The small yellow flowers appear during, or toward the end of winter, in opposite pairs along the entire length of the bare branches of the previous year's growth. Their narrow tubular corollas open out into 5 flat, open lobes.
Cultivation Although this is a rustic, cold-resistant plant, it likes to be in a sunny position to prepare for its early flowering; in dry weather it should be kept well-watered, especially in the autumn. It prefers warm, clayey, damp soil. The plant should be pruned when flowering has finished and, if new branches are desired, it should be cut back to ground level.
Winter protection In a cold climate winter jasmine can be covered with plastic sheeting or small branches of conifers.
Propagation By cuttings in August, by simple layering in the autumn, by seed in September. It can be transplanted in spring and autumn. It is very hardy in the British Isles.
Other species *J. mesnyi*, of Chinese origin, has large, yellow, semidouble flowers and thrives in the sun. *J. humile*, originating from the Himalayas, has scented yellow flowers.

---

140 JASMINUM POLYANTHUM
Jasmine

U.S. zone 9

Family Oleaceae.
Place of origin China.
Description A graceful, elegant evergreen climber with long, slender branches up to about 20 ft. (6 m.) long. Its opposite, green, pinnate and lobate leaves are about 4 in. (10 cm.) long with 5–7 leaflets. The tubiform flowers with their star-like corolla are sweetly scented; the pink buds open into white flowers grouped in panicles of axillary inflorescences but are not long-lasting since all the flowers open at about the same time.
Cultivation *J. polyanthum* needs a sunny position or, if in semishade, plenty of light; in cooler areas it should be grown against a wall for shelter or in a tub. It does not like acid soil and needs regular watering as it cannot tolerate dryness. Any non productive branches should be pruned out in the autumn to encourage new flowering growth, and the racemes that have flowered should also be removed in the summer.
Winter protection Plants in containers should be put under cover in a cool but sheltered place.
Propagation By simple layering in the autumn, by cuttings from the current year's growth in the autumn.
Other species *J. dispermum*, from the Himalayas, semiever-green, with abundant fragrant, white, pink-flushed flowers. *J. grandiflorum* has large flowers, which are pink when in bud; it has a climbing, bushy habit. *J. officinale*, a climber from China and the Himalayas, the hardiest of the genus, has medicinal properties and is particularly valued for the essence that is obtained from its little, white, scented flowers.

141 LONICERA × AMERICANA

Family Caprifoliaceae.
Place of origin Europe.
Description An evergreen climbing plant that was produced by crossing *L. caprifolium* with *L. etrusca*. It is a popular garden plant because of its hardiness, the abundance of its leaves and the delicate perfume of its flowers. It grows to a length of 20 ft. (6 m.) or more, wherever there is something for it to grow over, such as a tree trunk or wall. Its leaves are opposite, green on the upper surface and glaucous beneath; they vary in shape, those on the stems being elliptic while those at the top are small and ovate; the leaves that surround the flowering corymbs are connate. Its flowers, which have long tubes with a bilabiate corolla, are dark red in the bud and white and buttery-yellow when fully open; about 2 in. (5 cm.) long; their perfume becomes stronger in the evening to attract butterflies on which they rely for fertilization. After flowering, clusters of small red berries, glossy and rather like polished coral, are produced and are a welcome source of food for birds. The generic name is dedicated to the 16th-century German botanist Adam Lonitzer.
Cultivation *Lonicera* can withstand frost and adapts to any position and type of soil although it likes moisture and, above all, to have its base in shade. Its head can be damaged by wind. A dressing of manure and a good mulch of leafmold in early spring benefits flowering. It also grows well in tubs.
Propagation By seed in the spring or autumn; also by simple layering, by air layering and by cuttings.

---

142 MANDEVILLA SUAVEOLENS
Chilean Jasmine

Family Apocynaceae.
Place of origin Argentina.
Description A sweetly scented deciduous climber that grows to a considerable length. The woody stem transudes a sweet, white latex at each axil from which the opposite leaves spring; these are acuminate and cordate, 2–4 in. (5–10 cm.) long. The white flowers are tubiform, about 2 in. (5 cm.) long, with 5 petals and gathered into axillary racemes; they are particularly fragrant at dusk. In hot climates, where flowering is more prolific, the fading flowers develop into long pods containing numerous seeds.
Cultivation *Mandevilla* is suitable for hedging and to cover pergolas and walls. In colder areas these should be south-facing since it cannot withstand frost, however, the base must be kept in the shade. It is ideal for warm seaside gardens, where an east-facing position is preferable; excessive heat can cause blotches and other damage to the leaves. In cooler areas it also grows well in large containers. It should not be watered in the winter. It grows in any type of soil. Any branches that have not flowered should be cut out when the flowering season is over.
Winter protection Necessary where prolonged frosts are possible. In cold areas it requires greenhouse protection.
Propagation By seed in February or September, by cuttings in the summer.
Other species *M. splendens*, with pink or carmine flowers.

143 PARTHENOCISSUS QUINQUEFOLIA
Virginia Creeper, American Ivy　　　　　　**U.S. zone 4**

Family Vitaceae.
Place of origin Northeastern America.
Description A self-clinging deciduous climber that grows to about 100 ft. (30 cm.) with the aid of its branched tendrils, which become modified into disk-shaped suction cups on a wall. The palmate leaves, about 4 in. (10 cm.) long, have 5 slender-tipped, serrate leaflets, which are grayish-green on the lower surface; the upper surface is red in the spring, green in the summer and brilliant shades of golden, red and scarlet in the autumn, creating a very showy effect. The flowers are inconspicuous and develop into round, bluish-black berries.
Cultivation It is a hardy plant, grown to cover walls, gateways, pergolas and hedges. It grows quickly in any type of soil, preferably moist and well-fertilized. A sunny position will improve its autumnal colours. It is frost-resistant. Young plants should be cut right back after planting and provided with a support. Virginia creeper can be pruned to remove any frost-damage or to train it in a particular direction. Keep well-watered in dry weather.
Propagation By cuttings in the summer, by simple layering in the spring or autumn. It can be transplanted from October–March.
Other species *P. henryana*, originating from China, is less frost-resistant. *P. himalayana*, likes a sheltered, sunny position. *P. tricuspidata*, (*Ampelopsis tricuspidata, Vitis inconstans*), a self-clinging deciduous climber with adhesive suction pads; its alternate trilobate leaves turn bright crimson in the autumn; it is not frost-resistant and requires a sunny, sheltered position.

---

144 PASSIFLORA CAERULEA
Blue Passion Flower　　　　　　**U.S. zone 8**

Family Passifloraceae.
Place of origin Brazil.
Description A most striking evergreen climber, this passion flower is the hardiest and well-suited to most gardens. It climbs vigorously along a support for about 6–7 ft. (2 m.) by means of twining tendrils and can be used to decorate pergolas, gateways and walls. Its palmate leaves have 5–7 lobes, up to 6 in. (15 cm.) long, green on the upper surface and glaucous beneath. The star-like axillary flowers, 2⅜–4 in. (6–10 cm.) across and faintly scented grow singly; their corolla has 5 sepals with 5 pinkish-white petals interspersed and a purple-fringed corona in the center of which is the long pistil with 3 stigmas and 5 stamens rayed horizontally. The common name derives from its resemblance to the crown of thorns and the nails in the crucifixion of Christ. The oval, orange fruits are very decorative.
Cultivation It prefers loamy, moist soil, only lightly fertilized. The passion flower withstands frost unless prolonged. It likes a sunny, airy position. It thrives in a small pot, where it will grow in tight spirals. Keep well-watered in spring and summer. Hard pruning in the late winter encourages the growth of new flowering branches.
Winter protection If frost should be prolonged, the plant should be covered with plastic sheeting and its base protected with straw, peat or ashes.
Propagation By seed in March–April, by cuttings in July, by simple layering.

145 POLYGONUM BALDSCHUANICUM
(syn. *Bilderdykia baldschuanica*
Fallopia baldschuanica)

U.S. zone 5

Family Polygonaceae.
Place of origin Afghanistan, west Pakistan, south U.S.S.R.
Description A woody, climbing plant that grows quickly and vigorously, reaching about 40 ft. (15 m.) overall. Its branches, brownish when young, fall in a spiral. The numerous nodes on the stems are typical of the genus. Its alternate leaves are heart-shaped or cordate-sagittate, up to 3½ in. (9 cm.) long, smooth and tender, and borne on long stalks. The perfumed white flowers grouped in terminal or axillary clusters, shade to pink; although insignificant individually they are collectively very decorative when fully in flower.
Cultivation Its rapid and continuous growth makes it an ideal plant for covering large areas such as pergolas, roofs, gateways, fences or arches, even if they are in the shade. It always needs a support. It is very hardy and frost-resistant provided that it is in a sunny, sheltered position. In a mild climate it grows well even in the shade. Immediately after planting, the young shoots should be cut back a little to enable the roots to become established and to make the plant branch out. It likes moist, well-fertilized, open ground. The whole plant should be trimmed after flowering to keep it from becoming unwieldy.
Winter protection In cold areas its base should be protected with straw, matting or leaves.
Propagation By cuttings in the autumn, by seed in March, by simple layering.
Other species *C. aubertii (Fallopia aubertii, Bilderdykia aubertii)* (Russian Vine, Mile-a-Minute), slightly larger leaves.

146 ROSA MULTIFLORA
(syn. *R. polyantha*)

U.S. zone 6

Family Rosaceae.
Place of origin Japan and Korea.
Description A climber, scrambler rose that can reach a height of up to 30 ft. (10 m.). Its white flowers are not very large; the light red fruits are small and ovoid.
Cultivation This rose grows in any soil but it prefers ground that is consistently rich in organic material, clayey rather than loose, and well-worked. Ideally the soil needs to be fairly alkaline. Bare-root plants should be set out in spring or autumn in deep holes that have been well dug and enriched with well-rotted manure. Pruning is done in the autumn and spring to remove dead, weak and thin branches. Long new shoots should be left to replace the old, weak ones. The old main branches can be shortened by one-third and their lateral branches cut back to 1–2 buds.
Propagation By grafting, by cuttings, by air layering.
Other species *R. wichuraiana*, with small white fragrant flowers. *R. sempervirens*, tender and fragrant white flowers. *R. arvensis*, a vigorous trailer, has sweetly scented white flowers.

147 SOLANUM WENDLANDII

Family Solanaceae.
Place of origin Costa Rica.
Description A deciduous climbing plant with exuberant summer flowering, it extends to about 23 ft. (7 m.) in length. Although its stem appears fragile, it can climb upward or tumble over a wall. Its bright green leaves are simple and ovate on the upper branches but pinnate and lobate on the lower ones. There are curved spines on the venation of the underside of each leaf. The light blue-violet flowers are 2 in. (5 cm.) across with a yellow center; the flowers are grouped in large, dense racemes that may also be pendulous, but they do not all come into bloom at the same time. Its small, round fruits ripen only in hot countries.
Cultivation *S. wendlandii* needs a warm climate, but it also grows in pots or the greenhouse. It likes loamy, well-drained, non-clayey soil and a sunny position. It offers little resistance to the cold but regenerates quite easily. To encourage new growth and aid flowering, damaged branches should be removed in early spring and untidy or weak ones shortened. A winter dressing of manure and regular watering in dry weather also benefit the plant considerably.
Winter protection The plant should be well mulched to protect it from the cold. Plants in pots should be put under cover.
Propagation By cuttings in the summer, by seed in the spring, by simple layering.
Other species *S. crispum*, from Chile, is hardy and semievergreen with purple flowers. *S. pensile*, with violet flowers, needs a warm climate and plenty of water. *S. jasminoides*, a semievergreen climber with light blue-white, star-like flowers.

---

148 WISTERIA FLORIBUNDA

Family Leguminosae.
Place of origin Eastern Asia, eastern U.S.
Description A climbing plant that can grow to about 33 ft. (10 m.). The woody stem twines in a clockwise direction. Its compound leaves, up to 10 in. (25 cm.) long, have 11–19 leaflets. Its flowers open gradually from the base of the plant upward at the same time as the leaves emerge; the pendulous racemes up to 10 in. (25 cm.) in length, are mauve and pleasantly perfumed. Smaller racemes appear in the summer in a secondary bloom period. In warmer areas fruits in the form of flat, green, pendulous pods appear quite late.
Cultivation Wisteria needs well-drained, loamy soil and a dressing of general fertilizer every autumn. The entire plant, including the roots, likes to be in the sun. After transplanting, keep it well-watered for the first few years; flowers will begin to appear after a year or two. Keep it pruned every year to encourage flowering; the lateral branches should be cut back to the fifth leaf in the summer and to the second bud in late winter. The vine needs a very sturdy support. Keep it away from house walls, otherwise the stems will grow under or into the pointing and tear it off.
Propagation By simple layering, cuttings in late summer.
Other species *W. sinensis* (Chinese Wisteria), from China, is distinguishable by its anti-clockwise twining and by its flowers, which all open at the same time. *W. venusta*, originating from Japan, has large white flowers. *W. floribunda* 'Alba,' has white flowers in racemes 1½–2 ft. (50–60 cm.) long.

GLOSSARY

achene a dry, indehiscent, one-seeded fruit.
aciculate needle-shaped.
acid a term used to describe soil with a low percentage of lime and a pH below 7.
acuminate terminating in a point.
agamic asexual; reproducing by means other than seeds.
air layering type of vegetative propagation carried out by means of a specially treated area of a branch, which is enclosed in a filmous sleeve until rooting takes place. The new plant can then be detached and planted.
alate winged.
alternate of leaves when they are arranged at different heights on the stem. Compare with the entry for **opposite**.
amplexicaul a leaf or broad bract that clasps the stem.
anemophilous wind-pollinated.
anther pollen-bearing part of the stamen.
arcuate bent in a bowlike curve.
aristate bearded.
axil the angle formed by a leaf or lateral branch with the stem.
bacciform berry-shaped.
berry a fleshy, indehiscent fruit containing several hard-coated seeds.
bilabiate an organ with two prominent parts rather like lips.
bipinnate a leaf that is twice pinnate.
bisexual a flower that contains both male organs (stamens) and female organs (pistils).
bract a modified leaf situated at the base of a flower stalk.
bud the initial phase of new organs of a plant – branches, leaves or flowers.
bullate having blisters.
bush a fairly small plant with numerous branches that spring from the base; almost synonymous with **shrub**.
bushy having the habit of a bush with numerous branches originating from a single root.
caducous not persistent; of sepals, falling off as the flower opens; of stipules, falling off as the leaves unfurl.
calcareous soil rich in calcium carbonate; alkaline, not acid.
calyx collective term for the sepals of a flower.
campanulate bell shaped.
capitulum type of inflorescence, as seen in the Compositae.
capsulate a dry dehiscent fruit that opens on ripening by parting of its valves; thus its seeds are dispersed.
carina the two lower petals of a papilionaceous flower; also known as the keel.
carpel a modified fertile floral leaf that, collectively, forms the pistil.
chlorosis yellowing of the leaves due mainly to mineral deficiencies or waterlogging.
ciliate having margins fringed with hairs.
clayey a soil type with a high proportion of clay.
climber a plant whose stem is unable to support it but which can climb upward by means of special vegetative features and by using whatever supports are available.
clump division reproduction of plants by dividing a crown or clump into two or more parts.
compost humus made up of a variety of decomposed materials.
cordate heart-shaped.

coriaceous of a semi-rigid consistency; leathery.

corolla the collective term for the petals of a flower.

corymb flat-topped or rounded flower head with the outermost flowers opening first.

culm stem of grasses.

cultivar a garden variety, or a form found in the wild and maintained as a clone in cultivation.

cutting a means of asexual propagation that consists of inserting parts (root, stem, leaf) of a plant into a suitable rooting medium; these will eventually produce roots and eventually new plants.

cyme a flat-topped or rounded flower head with the innermost flowers opening first.

deciduous used to describe leaves that fall at the end of the vegetative season.

dehiscent (of fruits) that open spontaneously on ripening to disperse the seeds.

dentate of a leaf margin that is sharply toothed.

denticulate with tooth-like projections.

dioecious bearing male flowers on one plant and female flowers on another.

divaricate to branch out, separate widely.

drupe a fruit with a fleshy middle and a single hard seed (kernel), the whole being enclosed in a tough outer skin.

elliptic in the shape of an ellipse, tapering at both ends with the broadest part across the middle.

evergreen a plant that seems to retain its leaves all the time but which is continually replacing them during the periods of vegetative rest.

fasciculate in clusters.

ferruginous rust-coloured; reddish-brown.

filament the stalk of the anther; together they form the stamen.

gamopetalous with petals partly or entirely fused to each other.

gamosepalous with sepals partly or entirely fused to each other.

glabrous smooth, without hair.

glandulous covered with hairs that emit a viscous fluid when touched.

grafting a system whereby a union is formed between plants of different species by means of notching and the insertion of a shoot; the shoot is intended to become the main feature although the basic stock is usually more robust and its growth has to be strictly controlled.

hardy plants tolerant of freezing temperatures.

herbaceous of a non-woody perennial, which dies down to the ground after flowering.

hermaphrodite male or female flowers in the same inflorescence.

heterophyllous a plant that bears more than one form of leaves.

hispid covered with long, stiff hairs.

humus organic consistuent of the soil created by decomposed plant and animal matter.

hybrid a cross between different species, subspecies or varieties.

imparipinnate a pinnate leaf with a single leaflet at the tip.

indehiscent not opening when ripe; i.e. a seedpod.

inflorescence the flowering part of the plant.

infructescence fruit formed from an inflorescence.

laciniate of leaves when the margin is cut into deep, narrow, and irregular strips.

lanceolate of leaves that are lance-shaped, tapering at each end.

layering see **air layering** and **simple layering**.

leaflet one division of a compound leaf.

legume a dry dehiscent fruit, typical of the leguminous plants, which splits open on both sides when ripe to disseminate the seeds.

liana a climbing and twining plant (usually tropical).

lobate (of leaves) divided into lobes.

manure organic fertilizer of animal origin.

monoecious a plant bearing both male and female flowers.

mulch a layer of humus, straw, dried leaves, peat, plastic sheeting, etc., spread around the base of plants as a protection against frost and to conserve moisture; it also helps to prevent weeds from growing.

node the point on a stem where the leaves arise.

nodose with knot-like protuberances.

obovate a reversed egg-shaped leaf, with the narrow part at the base.

opposite describes two leaves positioned opposite each other at each node.

ovary the lower part of the pistil containing the ovules.

ovate (of leaves) egg-shaped.

ovule the internal organ of the ovary that becomes a seed after fertilization.

palmate a leaf shaped like an outstretched hand with deep, fingerlike lobes.

papilionaceous butterfly-shaped flower, which is characteristic of one division of the Leguminosae.

pappus calyx modified into a downy or scaly material, often resembling a ring of fine hairs, to aid wind dispersal.

paripinnate a compound pinnate leaf with an even number of leaflets.

peat a material resulting from the decomposition of plants; it is commonly added to soil to make it lighter, more moisture-retentive and more nourishing.

pedicel the stalk of a single flower in a cluster.

peduncle stalk bearing a flower or a flower cluster.

persistent a leaf, bract, etc. that remains on a plant for more than one growing season.

petal one of the parts of a corolla.

petiole a leaf stalk.

pH the symbol used to express the acidity or alkalinity of soil; if the pH is equal to 7, the solution is neutral; if it is over 7, it is alkaline, and if less than 7, it is acid.

pilose covered with hair.

pinna the primary division of a pinnate leaf.

pinnate describes a leaf in which the leaflets are positioned on either side of a central stalk.

piriform pear-shaped.

pistil the female part of a flower consisting of the ovary, style and stigma.

pollen a collection of tiny grains that develop in the anthers and that contain the male gametes.

pollination the process of conveying pollen from the anther to the stigma.

procumbent growing along the ground; prostrate.

propolis a red or brown resinous substance produced by the buds of some plants and used as glue by the bees; in solution, it is a natural pesticide.

pruning the cutting away of branches or dead parts of a plant or the shortening of living branches to certain nodes; it is a skilled operation requiring some study.

pubescent covered with very short, soft hairs.

raceme a long inflorescence whose flowers get progressively shorter toward the end; the terminal flower is the last to open.

reniform kidney-shaped.

reticulate with veins arranged in a net-like form.

root the part of a plant that is generally underground and anchors it in the soil, absorbing the nutriment and moisture necessary for growth.

rostrate with a beak-like part.

rugose wrinkled.

sagittate shaped like an arrowhead.

samara an indehiscent fruit with a single seed equipped with a wing-like membrane to facilitate wind dispersal; e.g. a "key" from a maple.

sap a liquid that runs through plants and that constitutes their nutritive essence.

seed the reproductive organ of plants derived from the fertilized ovule and containing the embryo of a future plant.

sepals the calyx of a flower.

sericeous covered with soft down; silky.

serrate tooth-edged, like a saw.

sessile stalkless.

sheath basal part of some leaves that wraps around the branch or stem. A semi-tubular structure surrounding some part of a plant.

shoot young herbaceous growth that can be used for cuttings.

simple layering type of vegetative propagation achieved by pegging a flexible branch down to the ground where it will strike root after a certain time. The new plant can then be detached and planted.

species a basic category of classification. A species is composed of similar but distinct individuals that interbreed freely among themselves but not among other species.

spine a woody, sharp-pointed body.

stamens male organ of a flower.

stellate starlike.

stem the fundamental organ of a plant, above the roots, which serves to support all the other organs (branches, leaves, flowers) and to conduct the nutritive substances so that they will reach the extremities.

stigma the terminal part of the pistil that receives and stores the pollen.

striate slightly ridged or striped.

style the connective tissue linking the ovary to the stigma.

subcordate almost heart-shaped.

substrate the substances of which the soil is composed on which a plant will grow.

succulent a fleshy plant, typical of dry climates, that has the ability to retain large amounts of water in the leaves and stem.

sucker a branch that develops from the roots of a plant.

suffrutescent a plant with a woody structure in its lower parts on which it produces tender shoots of a herbaceous consistency.

taxa refers to a taxonomic group of any rank, e.g. genus, species, cultivar, etc.

tendril a threadlike (filiform) organ derived from a leaf or branch, which is able to attach itself to a support and twine round on itself, thus supporting a weak stem.

tetragonal having 4 angles and 4 convex faces.

tomentose (of leaves) densely covered with short, soft, matted wooly hairs.

transplanting the transfer of a plant from one site to another.

trifoliate divided into three leaflets.

trigonal triangular in cross section.

tripartite   a leaf divided into 3 segments almost to the base.

trunk   the woody stem of a tree.

turbinate   shaped like a top or inverted cone.

tubiform   cylindrical.

umbel   an inflorescence in which the flowers are arranged like the spokes of an umbrella.

umbelliferous   a plant bearing umbels.

umbilicate   having a navel-like depression.

undulate   (of leaves) with a wavy margin.

unisexual   a flower that only has male (stamens) or female (pistil) organs.

urceolate   pitcher-shaped, with a large body and small mouth, usually describing a corolla.

variegated   a leaf or flower with markings or stripes in different colors.

variety   a unit of classification below species or subspecies, composed of individuals differing from the species in very minor characteristics.

velutinate   with a velvety surface.

verticil   an arrangement of leaves grouped around a node; a whorl.

verticillate   arranged in verticils (whorls).

vexillum   the large petal standing up at the back of a papilionaceous flower.

INDEX

(The numbers refer to the corresponding entry in the book.)

Picture sources

Introduction

L. Cretti, Milan: 32, 35, 49; Fotoflora-A. Ferrari, Milan: 16, 19, 36-37, 41, 44-45; Jacana, Paris: 33; Moreschi, Sanremo: 17, 38; G. Neri, Perderau, Milan: 8-9; V. Pigazzini, Monza: 11, 28, 29; F. Speranza, Milan: Ken Strighton 12-13.

Entries

Ardea, London: 24b, 46b, 50, 95c, 111b; E. Arnone, Milan: 35, 42, 89, 106b, 126; R. C. Balfour, Chelmsford, Essex: 32, 62a; L. Cretti, Milan: 1, 6, 7, 11, 12ab, 15, 16, 24c, 29b, 36, 41, 56, 68, 69, 78, 83b, 87, 92, 96, 107, 108, 110ab, 112, 117a, 118ab. 125, 130b, 132, 143; Foto Lamontagne: 146; S. Frattini, Milan: 28a; Jacana, Paris: 5a, 20b, 21b, 24a, 28b, 30a, 45, 46a, 74, 75, 77, 82a, 90b, 95ab, 98a, 100, 109b, 121c, 138b; Lanzani, Milan: 4, 64, 94, 101a, 120a, 124; Moreschi, Sanremo: 25ab, 33, 38, 39, 55, 57, 63, 65, 71, 80, 120b, 122, 123, 128, 129, 133a, 134, 140, 142, 147, 148; Nature, Chamalières: 18, 20a, 21a, 27, 52b, 82b, 84b, 90a, 101b, 114ab, 117c, 119b, 127, 133b, 138c; V. Pigazzini, Monza: 59, 79, 121b; A. Prati, Trento: 131; H. Smith, Horticultural Photographic Collection, Chelmsford, Essex: 5b, 8, 26, 29a, 34, 37b, 47, 49a, 52ac, 53b, 58, 61, 62b, 66, 70, 73b, 86, 90c, 97, 103, 106a, 117b, 136, 145; M. Warren, Photos Horticultural, Ipswich, Suffolk: 2, 3, 5c, 9, 10, 13, 14, 17ac. 19, 20c, 21c, 22, 23, 28c, 30b, 31, 37a, 40, 43, 44, 48, 49b, 51, 53a, 54, 60, 67, 72, 73a, 76, 81, 82c, 83a, 84a, 85, 88, 91, 93, 98b, 99, 102, 104, 105, 109a, 111a, 113, 114c, 115, 116, 119a, 121a, 130a, 135, 137, 138a, 139, 141, 144.

The photographs at the beginning of each section are from: E. Arnone, Milan (Shrubs); Jacana, Paris/A. Carraro (Small and ornamental trees); V. Pigazzini, Monza (Opposite title page); M. Warren, Photos Horticultural, Ipswich, Suffolk (Climbing plants).